A Little Edge of Darkness

A Boy's Triumph over Dyslexia

of related interest

Children with Special Needs
Assessment, Law and Practice –
Caught in the Acts, 3rd edition
John Friel
ISBN 1 85302 280 2

Young Adults with Special Needs
Assessment, Law and Practice –
Caught in the Acts
John Friel
ISBN 1 85302 231 4

Dyslexia – How Would I Cope?
3rd edition
Michael Ryden
ISBN 1 85302 385 X

A Little Edge of Darkness

A Boy's Triumph over Dyslexia

Tanya and Alexander Faludy

Jessica Kingsley Publishers
London and Bristol, Pennsylvania

The right of Tanya and Alexander Faludy to be identified as authors of this work has been asserted by them in accordance with the Copyright, Designs and Patents Act 1988.

First published in the United Kingdom in 1996 by
Jessica Kingsley Publishers Ltd
116 Pentonville Road
London N1 9JB, England
and
1900 Frost Road, Suite 101
Bristol, PA 19007, U S A

Copyright © 1996 Alexander and Tanya Faludy
Cover photograph © 1994 The News

Library of Congress Cataloging in Publication Data
Faludy, Tanya, 1957-
A little edge of darkness / Tanya Faludy and Alexander Faludy,
p.   cm.
ISBN 1-85302-357-4 (alk. paper)
1. Faludy, Alexander, 1983- . 2. Dyslexic children–Education–
Great Britain–Case studies. 3. Dyslexic children–Great Britain–
Biography. I. Faludy, Alexander, 1983- . II. Title.
LC4710.G7F35   1996
371.91'44--dc20   95-41377
                                                        CIP

British Library Cataloguing in Publication Data
Faludy, Tanya
Little Edge of Darkness
I. Title II. Faludy, Alexander
371.9144

ISBN 1-85302-357-4

Printed and Bound in Great Britain by
Cromwell Press, Melksham, Wiltshire

To my parents, Alexander's grandparents,
George and Eileen Spencer, without whose
help all of this would not have been possible

Contents

Chronology

February	1983	Alexander born.
February	1987	Emily born.
Spring	1988	Alexander joins the pre-prep.
Throughout	1989	Momentous events in Eastern Europe.
Summer	1990	Alexander is diagnosed as dyslexic.
Autumn	1990	Joins MENSA and we move into our new house.
Autumn	1991	Begins lower school.
Summer	1992	Passes GCSE. Visits Eurodisney.
Summer	1993	Andrew, Alexander and I visit Hungary.
Summer	1994	Alexander visits Hungary, passes 'A' level, and enrols with the Open University as the youngest Arts undergraduate in Britain.
Winter	1994	Leaves school.
Spring	1995	Open University Course begins.
Autumn	1995	Begins at Milton Abbey.

Foreword

This book combines in one volume a biography and auto-biography. It tells the story of Alexander's life to date from a double perspective: mine, as I gradually became aware of his strange combination of dyslexic handicap and exceptional intellectual ability; and his, as he recounts first hand the isolation felt by a child who, whilst appearing physically normal, is progressively and puzzlingly rejected.

I always wrote my chapter first, but did not show it to him — I just indicated the time span covered. While my account details the mechanics of the obstacles which had to be overcome, his tells the story from within the mind of a dyslexic child. The different points of view will, we hope, provide interest for the reader, giving a rounded description of the problems we have faced in the last few years. By definition, because the book focuses on his educational development, it by no means gives a full picture of our lives: details about our family and friends are therefore sparse.

Alexander's achievements were forged against a background of personal difficulty, and frequently, I regret to say, external resistance. However, I would like to thank all those who helped, whether they are named individually in the book or not. In particular I am grateful to: Dr Paul Dean, for his encouragement in general of Alexander over a very long period of time; Mr Robin Freeland, educational psychologist, whose observations have been so influential in developing our thought processes; Mrs Elisabeth Wade, for her invaluable assistance, both through tuition and transcription at 'A' level; my parents for their help all along, with just about everything imaginable; and Andrew and Clare Phillips, close friends, who provided crucial support in what seemed impossibly difficult moments.

Tanya Faludy

CHAPTER ONE

From Bewilderment to Breakthrough

Like most expectant mothers I tried to do the best for my unborn baby. In my case, it took the form of healthy eating, not drinking alcohol, and attending natural childbirth classes with my husband, Andrew. We pretended to be trees bending in the wind, and breathed deeply, but nothing can quite prepare you for the birth of your first child. The second stage of labour lasted two hours; my son had the cord wrapped twice around his neck and was a hideous bluish-purple colour at birth. As he was pronounced fit and healthy, however, any misgivings were dismissed as I held our newborn in my arms.

Andrew and I had pored for hours over books of babies' names, never quite being able to agree. So in the end we reached a compromise – he could pick the names of any boys we had, and I would choose those for the girls. We called him Sándor – a continuity with the past, reflecting Andrew's Hungarian origins – but changed it to the English translation – Alexander – as we realised that people's difficulties in pronunciation could make things awkward and difficult for our son. Having heard some recent cases of parents calling their children after all the players in a football team, or a polysyllabic Welsh railway station, we were very keen that our child should have a name which enabled him to fit in.

When he was a few weeks old, however, we became aware that he was, in fact, different. Andrew and I were chatting as I breast fed Alexander when my nipple slipped out of his mouth with strange pop. We laughed. He looked into our eyes with a twinkle and smiled and laughed too, and then repeated the action. We couldn't believe it: he was sharing a joke already! Three years later we learned of the scope of his early cognition as he pointed to photographs of Andrew carrying him as a baby and said, 'I remember that I *wanted* to walk but I couldn't – you and mummy had to carry me'.

The essence of his nature was already becoming clear, for together with our perception of his early intelligence came that of an unusual clumsiness – a lack of coordination. He kept aiming at, and missing, the chiming multi-coloured fluffy ball that we had dangled from his carry cot. Later, my mother, who adores him, bought a Fisher Price activity center which he made attempts at mastering, failed, and thereafter lost interest in such toys. The attitudes of other parents who had attended the same ante-natal classes as us were condescending. They seemed to display the aptitude and dexterity of their children while tacitly dismissing Alexander as rather backward but very sweet. I had the strange feeling at mother and baby get-togethers that Alexander was invited, either to make up the numbers, or out of politeness, but that as he wasn't in the forefront of visible development, he was of little real interest to the rest.

Our concern grew as Alexander failed to master other infant toys, such as building bricks, simple jigsaw puzzles and colouring books – everything, in fact, that required a coordination between the hand and the eye, although he could walk at eleven months and talk soon after. We constantly expressed our concerns to health visitors, but were made to feel that we were being rather over-sensitive, for we were assured that all was well, as children develop at different rates and that we must not be so anxious; he would catch up in the end.

Meanwhile, as time progressed and he started to attend playgroups, music clubs and tumbletots, Alexander stuck out like a sore thumb, precisely because, while there was nothing visibly wrong with him, there was an awkwardness which set him apart from the others. A playgroup video was made: it showed children painting, sticking, gluing – being physically involved with each other and the play equipment on a take it or leave it basis. Alexander, however, could be seen wandering around deep in thought, observing the behaviour of others, tentatively having a go on things now and then, but seeming strangely distant from the whole procedure. We recently showed him this video and he told us that he clearly remembered his feelings: he couldn't work out what the right thing to do was. He said that he could recall running around now and then, so that it would look as though he was playing, but really he felt quite at a loss in such situations.

Andrew and I both worked but we were very lucky in our child care arrangements. My parents looked after Alexander, and he was secure in the extended family environment of parents, grandparents, his great-grandmother and great great aunt. As college lecturers, however, Andrew and I were able to arrange our timetables (by working some twilight and evening classes) in such a way as to involve Alexander in as wide a variety of playgroups as if I had been at home full time. On one afternoon, when Andrew was trying to be accepted at a mother and toddler group, he was severely criticised for the fact that Alexander still used a teacher beaker, whereas all the rest drank their orange juice from cups. A particularly forceful matron made it clear that she regarded his lack of progress as our fault for retarding him. 'Open cups and Alexander really don't go together,' Andrew pleaded, as the drink was forced on Alexander with the statement that the child had to be the same as the rest, and if we didn't try he wouldn't learn. He promptly drenched his clothes and had to be taken home. Thus by not accepting him on his own terms, she had rendered him unable to participate in the group at all that day.

Such incidents reinforced our growing conviction that *we* were the ones who understood our child; that received wisdom was inappropriate to his individual condition. The problem was, however, that we didn't know either how to help him with his difficulties, or how to find something that he could do that would give him as much pleasure as creating models out of play dough gave other children.

And then came the breakthrough when Alexander was three. Like most things that are consequential in our lives it happened by accident. It was a spin-off of an unconnected trait in my personality. I used to love the Sales, and like my mother, got a special delight from the impulse buying of bargains. One day, as I walked through Woolworths I saw a large special offer sign over children's story tapes – all half price – 99p. Such tapes, which whilst common now, were relatively novel ten years ago. I bought the lot – *Dr. Snuggles, Teddy Robinson, Portland Bill, Postman Pat, Thomas the Tank Engine*... Andrew was suitably dismayed as I struggled home with my latest bag of acquisitions, and jokingly confided in a visiting friend that my hobbies were shopping and talking on the telephone. Little did we know that the tapes were to change Alexander's life.

I gave him his first story tape to listen to in bed that night. He loved it and demanded to hear it through twice. He wasn't able to turn the cassette over himself, however, as he was too clumsy, so every half hour we would be summoned to do the honours. In the middle of the night Andrew and I were reluctantly roused from our slumbers by an insistent voice calling from the next bedroom.

'Wake up you two. I've got something to tell you.'

Our drowsy compliance was transformed into gripped amazement as Alexander started to recite – verbatim – for a whole hour the stories he had listened to earlier.

The next morning – half wondering if we had dreamt the strange nocturnal recitation, I asked Alexander if he could tell me those stories again whilst Andrew stood by with the tape recorder. He was only too willing to do so. It still brings a lump to my throat as I listen to the eager voice on that first tape piping with gleeful emphasis: '...as Thomas *whoooshed* into the station.'

+++++

Alexander was happy and fulfilled. His chief pleasure was listening to stories and learning new tapes by heart. At last he had found something that entertained him. He was also a source of entertainment for others. I remember leaving him in the kiddie corner of a bookshop one day while I browsed nearby, only to find a group of adults listening in amazement as he appeared to read aloud a fairly complex book with theatrical intonation and gestures to the assembled audience.

'Denizens of the North unite!' he shouted with a flourish of the arm. I didn't let on that he had listened to the story the night before.

As a family, we'd hunt for new tapes to amuse him, and in the mornings when he arrived at my parents' house, if we had dropped hints during the car journey, he would hurry to his bedroom there to see if a surprise tape awaited him. He would then take great delight in amusing his relatives with a happy recital of what he had heard. It was interesting to watch him during such performances, for, if someone interrupted him, or he had to go to the toilet, before he resumed he could be seen scanning his brain for exactly the right place: it was like pressing 'search' on the video. He seemed to have the exact audio equivalent of a photographic memory, but he also understood and enjoyed the material he listened to.

Alexander's relish of the individual words in his tapes expanded his vocabulary rapidly. There is a line said by Diesel in one of the *Thomas the Tank Engine* stories that goes something like this: 'Disgusting! Despicable! Disgraceful!' Alexander delighted in the sound of these words and asked us to tell him more which meant the same thing, and would apply them appropriately – if somewhat precociously – in everyday conversation. His new-found joy in words was therefore not restricted to recitation. He adopted at times a precision of definition which was metaphorical in its resonance.

One morning when aged about three and a half he tried to persuade us that it was time to get up.

'Wake up! 'Tis morning!' he shrilled. (It was about five thirty and pitch black.)

We replied that it wasn't – but he called back in triumph: 'Yes it is. I can see a little edge of darkness stealing away from the window pane.' We got up!

Aware that Alexander had a considerable oral ability, I decided to seek advice from the experts on how to develop his potential. I wrote outlining his condition to a local adviser for English and was disillusioned when I did not receive a reply. I kept on buying the tapes. By this time he was attending an independent teaching nursery school and it soon became apparent that he couldn't form his letters or numbers – he found it impossible to copy or recognise the simple shapes that others mastered with ease. He retreated into his own fictional world and his teacher summoned us for a concerned chat: 'I don't know what's wrong with Alexander – he can't write the number three no matter how patient I am with him – all he does when I try is to stand up and talk about engines!'

Around this time he was particularly friendly with a little boy who lived nearby, but I always found visits to his house disturbing – it was almost as if his mother would be setting up situations to show what her son could do and mine could not – Michael would be neatly colouring inside the lines and Alexander would be offered an expensive colouring book to do a page. He would scribble over it with what seemed at times like a deliberately wilful carelessness and I would receive sympathetic smiles. Then, out would come such humiliating torments as the puzzles – the lego, the chalks and easel upon which Michael would write his name. His delighted mother would then ask if Alexander would like a try. If it hadn't been that the two boys were so friendly I would have curtailed these visits. One day she decided to get out some books – Alexander immediately took one from her hand and said, 'Ah, I know that story,' and recited it as he pointed to the appropriate pictures.

'There he goes poll-parroting again,' she sighed.

This has been the typical attitude that we have constantly come up against over the years: people are all too keen to criticise Alexander for what he cannot do, but very few have been able to credit him for his strengths.

+-+-+-+-+-+

It was as he approached the age of four that the problems that we were going to have to face with his schooling emerged. There are, by reputation, two very good independent schools that admit boys in Portsmouth. One we had put his name down for at birth; the other, run by de la Salle brothers we had become drawn to after visits and open evenings because of what seemed a warm environment and concerned attitude. I was expecting our second child when I took him for interview at this school. Filled with a proud nervous excitement, I handed Alexander over at the door and returned two hours later to collect him. No hint of his performance was given at the time, but we were told to await the results in the post.

Our daughter, Emily, was born a few days later. As he had been an only child for years, we anticipated some sort of negative reaction from Alexander but he surprised us by behaving impeccably. Andrew was suspicious and asked him why he was being so good about it all. He replied: 'I did not want to spoil your day, Daddy. I have saved the day!' We were impressed by his thoughtfulness – it seemed remarkable to us that one so young could think a situation through and see it from the perspective of others.

A week later the delightful oasis of the after-glow of birth was shattered by the arrival of a letter from the school saying that it could not offer Alexander an immediate place because of his lack of motor control. Andrew and I were invited for a discussion. We brought some of the tapes with us to show what he could do and were shown drawings of people that Alexander had done to demonstrate to us what he could not. I was actually quite impressed by his attempts – they were better than any of his I had seen. A compromise was reached – if we could get him to write his name correctly within the next six weeks he would be offered a place for the following year.

The following weeks were a ghastly foretaste of our numerous attempts to accommodate Alexander to the conventional demands of the education system. I practised letter formation with him every day, and every day he would write his name differently to the point where Andrew and I (between ourselves only) would indulgently refer to him as Axle Faludy.

The weeks passed, and he somehow managed to write his name in a way which satisfied the school, although it was made clear to us that his lack of motor control was still considered to be a great problem. He wasn't given a place, but put on a mysterious thing called 'the waiting list'. How long we were supposed to wait we never found out.

The implication from all quarters seemed to be that we were doing something wrong with him. Even my family, whilst enjoying his vocabulary, stories, memory and conversation, began to query the advisability of letting him listen to so many tapes. The general opinion seemed to be that listening to stories must be what was stopping him from reading and recognising the shapes of letters on the page. We were not convinced, for the tapes were in addition to other conventionally recognised educational stimuli: they were in no way exclusive.

+++++

It was at this point that we began to be worried about the way that other children treated him. I was for a while involved in a reciprocal meeting arrangement from nursery with another mother. One day I noticed that Alexander hadn't been his usual vocal self, so I cuddled him and asked how he was getting on with the lady's two boys. He raised his large blue eyes to mine and said, 'It's okay mummy – I can manage most of the time, but I get scared when they press my head on a chair and sit on top of it'. So the bullying had begun, along with a growing sense of guilt in me that I wasn't around to look after my little boy when he had problems and needed me – a feeling that I'm sure many working mothers share.

While still waiting for him to enter the de la Salle college, we had a phone call from the school that we had enrolled him for years previously. Not keen to go through interviews again, I was going to turn down the offered appointment, but my mother persuaded me to take him, as she had always maintained that it was the best school in the city.

The interview was a tremendous success. The school looked at very young children's potential and did not necessarily expect them to be able to read or write fluently before admission. Indeed, the method of assessment was by means of an oral comprehension, which of course he sailed through. Alexander's delighted comment when Andrew told him that he had passed was –

'Well, I got in there without any difficulty, didn't I, Daddy?'

> It was to be his last educational success for years to come – his talents would not again be recognised in a formal manner until his oral method of presentation was accepted when he passed GCSE in English Literature at the age of nine.

Alexander's own account of the period covered in this chapter follows.
Like all his work it was dictated onto tape and transcribed.

Alexander's Account:

This is not a complete autobiography but a concentration on those aspects of my life I can recall which later could come to be seen as early manifestations of my dyslexic problems and my escape into literature. What I remember most is a feeling which permeated the whole of my early life. It was a sense, right from the beginning, when I started to socialise with other children, that I was in some way different. It isn't something that I can pinpoint as being at a certain time, in a certain place, in a certain year, on a certain occasion, but something that was part of me.

Like many babies, I felt frustration at not being able to walk, but this frustration was not something that was openly expressed, rather something that went on inside my head. It wasn't a worded thought, but more emotions taking the place of thought, or moulding in with the neurological process.

This I feel shows the way I perceived myself while I was a baby: that is, I could understand emotions, and think by using them, and the associated experience and consequences, to learn how to walk and talk. The frustration, anger and perseverance that I felt at the time later came to form my character.

These emotions later formed a role during my nursery school period and when I was a toddler. For instance, the element of frustration formed itself into boredom, and the anger of physical inability became individuality. Unlike the other toddlers I *was* bored at the playgroup and, unlike the toddlers who were in a world which I didn't feel part of, I tried to stay with the adults I knew best, the friends of my grandmother and so on. And so I came to feel more of an observer than a participant: I sat and watched from a chair while the others played on the floor. This also made me feel that I wasn't the same, a feeling which had been there all the time, but which was only being realised bit by bit. At the time, of course, I couldn't understand what it was that made me different.

This also prevented me from making new friends because I was in a different world from my contemporaries and I was not perhaps interested in the same things, and because I had become shy, retreating into the circle that I knew well. I didn't really know *how* to make new friends, and so started to develop my own personality outside that of the group. I was becoming a stranger and an outsider to the other children.

A way in which I developed my own world, was by the use of tapes and television. I used to watch programmes like *Postman Pat* or *Thomas the Tank Engine*, and my parents bought me the audio tapes of one of the series and I would listen to them a few times and start reciting them over and over again to my relatives, some of the workers at my nursery school and to my small circle of friends. I was trying to involve them in and draw them deeper into my own world – to things that I was interested in. Most of them weren't able to comprehend, or to see the relevance of my enthusiasm. My nursery school teacher told my parents, 'He is a nice boy, but all he does is talk about trains', i.e. the Thomas the Tank Engine stories, and I can remember a teacher as I started reciting one of the stories saying, 'That's all very nice, but tell me about it later. Try and get on with your work.' The work she wanted of me was precisely what I couldn't achieve.

Through listening to these tapes I broadened my own imagination, introducing myself to new fields, new ways of life; for instance, on the lighthouse with Portland Bill. Another thing that came about because of listening to these tapes is that I took an interest in the way that words were expressed, not only because they conjured up a picture, but because they gave me ideas about how unfamiliar things tasted, how things looked and how things smelled. I wanted to try some of them; to see or experience the events expressed in the stories.

Perhaps the most important thing about these tapes for me, at the time anyway, was that they were my method of relief and escape. At playschool, other children were taught to read. They tried to teach *me*, but I was never any good at it, to begin with, and even when I did learn to read I was very slow and couldn't read books properly until much later than other children, around the age of seven. These tapes were being read by other people. They seemed more real to me than the print on the book, because they conjured up an image which the words on the page couldn't. They were my method of escape, going into my own world: they were my relief from people trying in vain to teach me how to write and read. These tapes ironically also had the effect of shoving me onto the periphery, because I couldn't actually be part of those stories, however much I tried to recreate them. So even in my own world, I was an outsider.

I remember that I often felt uncomfortable with other children's behaviour. I had a clear understanding of what was right and wrong, what was acceptable and not. I used to distance myself from the mischievious antics of others at nursery, for I could see the consequences beyond their actions – that they were going to get told off. By keeping away from trouble, I made myself unpopular.

I also became distanced from other children at playgroup and playschool because they bullied me. They could sense something odd about me, I suppose, like small children can, and so they started to tease and bully me, which got progressively worse as I got older. This put me off making new friends, because I didn't know what was going to happen. It made me more cautious – what I mean is, it cut me off from the group and from the new arrivals into the group, and so I was, in a way, silently excluded from them.

CHAPTER TWO

Creeping like a Snail

For many parents, I suppose that lavishing attention to detail on a first school uniform is a method of displacement for the loss felt as their child grows away from them. Care taken over his new clothes balances the realisation that one's baby is growing up: they are trophies in a rite of passage.

Alexander looked so smart in his grey shirt, shorts and jumper, a bright scarlet tie, grey ankle socks with a red band around the top, and black blazer rimmed in red braid and emblazoned on the breast pocket with a golden lion. His appearance was matched by an excitement and an eager desire to do his best.

The seeds of doubt were, however, sown after the first two days when the head teacher casually commented to Andrew after school that she did hope she had made the right decision in accepting Alexander, when we were so keen on the de la Salle school, for others were desperate for a place here. Just as the glow surrounding Emily's birth had been dimmed by the worry over Alexander's progress, so now Alexander's school career seemed to be under shadow, and he had only just begun.

We spent that evening going over what she could have meant. We had never mentioned our early interest in the other school to her, so what was she implying? Even if she did know, it was then an accepted practice for parents to keep their options open by putting their boys down for both schools. Our minds went down all sorts of pathways. I was all for speaking to the teacher, to find out just what she had meant, but Andrew insisted that we let the matter rest as Alexander would prove his own worth. However, it still remains a puzzle.

It was a matter of great concern to us that although he had several casual playmates from school, Alexander failed to make any close friends. I think the reason was to do with differing expectations of the nature of recreation. I once overheard a conversation between him and a boy who had come to play. They were both dressed as pirates, and I was delighted because I thought things were going splendidly until I heard the other boy, in exasperation, begging Alexander to stop talking about military techniques and pick up a cutlass and fight him. It seemed that Alexander gained greater pleasure from analysis than actual hands on play.

Alexander enjoyed being at school. He found the intellectual and physical environment exciting, the discipline firm but fair, and the teachers friendly. All seemed to be going well, until near the end of the first term, when his teacher had a concerned word with me after school one day. It seemed that Alexander had no fixed hand to write with. At first I found this idea exciting, and pondered whether there was a special flexibility in his brain which would allow him to explore reality in novel ways. It was soon made clear to me that this, together with his habit of writing words backwards, was a cause for concern, not jubilation. The initial feeling was, however, that the nature of his problems was such that, with perseverance, they could be overcome in time. His first report commented that Alexander had difficulty in achieving the level of control needed for letter formation but that it would develop with age and experience.

The next term a member of staff with special needs training did some diagnostic exercises with him, and Andrew and I were invited to a meeting with her, the head teacher, and his class teacher. Here, for the first time was the suggestion of the possibility that he might be dyslexic, but we were advised that the received wisdom was to wait until he was seven before having him tested. Alexander was only five, had been accepted by the best school in the city, but might possibly be dyslexic – we sought immediate re-assurance that, provided he was intellectually able, this potential disability should not affect his progress through the school. We were given no clear answer: this generated an insecurity in us, and we lived in a state of uncertainty concerning his future.

As I work in an English Department my colleagues had followed Alexander's development and delight in language with particular interest. At that time dyslexia awareness was not nearly as widespread as it is today: indeed, my own PGCE teacher training had not covered it at all. When I asked around to see if anyone had any useful information that would help me understand the condition, my Head of Department said that he had just received details of a one day conference on the subject, and although most of the teachers attending would be from the infant and junior sectors, he offered me the opportunity of representing our VIth form college.

The study day started with our being asked to compose a list of what we considered to be the symptoms of dyslexia. I thought of Alexander's problems and started my list:

- Mismatch between intellectual capacity and written work.
- Letters written backwards.
- Frustration with written work.
- Handwriting illegible.
- Left and right confusion.
- Lack of coordination.
- Good long term memory, but difficulty in sequencing and remembering lists.
- Frightful spelling.
- Clumsiness.

My points were similar to those of the others, constituting a classic profile of a dyslexic. From our list of symptoms, the senior educational psychologist leading the session gave us a working definition of dyslexia, or, as she called it, Specific Learning Difficulties (SLD). She said that children with SLD were those who, in the absence of sensory defect or overt organic damage, had an intractable learning problem in one or more of reading, writing, spelling and maths, and that they did not respond to normal teaching. For those children, early identification, sensitive encouragement and special teaching were necessary.

As the day progressed I learned of various, and what seemed to me rather complicated, remedial procedures, and understood *why* Alexander could not copy from the board because of the difficulty in transferring material from the horizontal to the vertical plane. I heard from teachers who fervently wished dyslexic children could be streamed according to their oral and reasoning abilities, if only there was the back-up in terms both of remedial teaching and the facilities occasionally to present work in alternative formats, such as letting the child see his messy work typed, or even accepting a piece of homework on tape.

Combined with my fascination at this glimpse into a world that Alexander so clearly inhabited was a growing frustration, and even anger, at the unfairness of some of the things the educational psychologist told us that dyslexics had to accept. Looking at the hurried notes I made at the time, certain points underlined and annotated with exclamation marks occasion a smile now:

'Realistically not going to reach potential!'

'Should not be an author.'

'*Should not* do "A" level English!'

It certainly never crossed my mind that one day I would be using these very notes that had caused me such distress, in the writing of a book in co-authorship with my dyslexic son, who *is* achieving his potential, having become the youngest person ever to pass 'A' level English Literature, at the age of eleven.

His next report highlighted what we were beginning to understand as the typical symptoms of dyslexia. In English, it said that Alexander had worked very hard, but still found difficulty with letter formation. This was unfortunately holding him back from achieving his full potential. In number work, the comments were equally revealing, stating that his lack of control slowed him down, whilst reaffirming that he had the ability, and that his mental work was good. It was such comments as these which would later form part of our thinking in liberating Alexander from letter formation, which had become an end in itself, to the development of his potential independently of it.

One of the teachers helped slow learners. Alexander had additional handwriting lessons and was put on a special reading scheme – the *Fuzzbuzz* books – which laboriously went over and over basic skills. We spent hours encouraging him as he struggled with his extra homework, but progress was slow, and didn't ever seem to be fully consolidated, for the problem was that he could not grasp the basics on which to build. His mind, infuriatingly, could not seem to accommodate the fundamental visual codes which underpin written communication.

At home, however, his intellectual abilities soared ahead. He progressed through C.S. Lewis's *Narnia* series at five, to J.R.R. Tolkien's *The Hobbit* six months later. Andrew read him the whole book during a week we spent in Devon at a National Trust Gatekeeper's cottage where there was no television, and sheep roamed in the front garden, munching on the greenery. Alexander hung on every word with wonder, and wept when Thorin Oakenshield died: 'There indeed lay Thorin Oakenshield, wounded with many wounds, and his rent armour and notched axe were cast upon the floor'. This book marked his transition from children's stories to the world of complex ideas of morality, the battle between good and evil, the uncomfortable idea of sacrifice, and the irreversible price of victory. He wanted us to read him the book again and again – it was then that we discovered the BBC audio collection, with its dramatic reconstructions of stories, not just readings of them: he could then listen to his heart's content.

The *Hobbit* tapes were cherished possessions for Alexander, and so for Christmas 1988, when he was five years and ten months old, my parents bought him the BBC edition of the *Lord of the Rings*. These tapes expanded the scope of his imaginative horizons, and as well as listening to tales, he began to want to invent them. He would compose whole stories, with clear structures and controlled development, in his head, and then dictate them to us. We copied out one of these stories neatly for him to show his teacher at school. She was very encouraging, and asked him to read it to the class. This well-intentioned gesture proved disastrous for Alexander, who became confused by not being able to read fluently the words so eagerly composed in his head. The other children teased him, saying that they didn't believe that he, who couldn't even write properly, could invent such a story.

At school, as at nursery, Alexander tended to inhabit a world in his head, where he was shielded from the taunts of his contemporaries. It was consequently at home where his true abilities shone. The prevailing birthday practice at the time was for each child to invite all the others in the class to a party, and this we duly arranged. On the actual day of his sixth birthday, however, we had a family celebration at my parents' house. After the candles were extinguished, we all jokingly called out, 'Speech, speech!' To our amazement, Alexander slowly rose, pulled himself to his full height, and began: 'Ladies and Gentlemen, we are gathered together today, in this very house, by the grace of God, in prosperity, to celebrate my sixth birthday...' He ended, 'Thank you all for making this such a happy occasion'.

When he had finished, we all stared at him in true appreciation, for a moment, before clapping, and then Andrew hastily pulled a scrap of paper from his pocket and wrote down what he could remember. Unfortunately the fragment above is all that remains, but it is representative of the quality and tone of the rest.

At times, Alexander's precocious enjoyment of texts aimed at the predominantly teenage market led to our having to explain to him at an early age concepts that we would not have contemplated broaching until much later. Having a conversation was, and still is, his favourite recreation. Emily, when given the choice, will like to play a game, whereas Alexander will say, 'I heard an interesting item on the radio the other day. What do you think about...?'

One day Alexander and Andrew were chatting in the kitchen when I was summoned: 'Alexander wants to know what "SEX APPEAL" is, Tanya – this is your department, I believe, please tell him!' my bemused husband wryly requested.

I explained that men and women felt an attraction towards each other which made them want to cuddle and kiss and asked why he wanted to know.

'Well,' he replied, 'in *The Hitchiker's Guide to the Galaxy,* Arthur Dent says of the Vogons, "I wish I had a daughter so I could forbid her to marry one". Ford Prefect replies, "You wouldn't need to. They've got as much sex appeal as a road accident".'

Alexander came to develop a real enjoyment of the abstract humour in this recording, but it was totally alien to the concepts of his contemporaries who later came to talk about such books at school at about the age of eleven. Over the next few years, Alexander would further this aspect of his mental exercise with tapes such as *The Long Dark Tea-Time of the Soul, The Foundation Trilogy,* and *Operation Lunar.*

At this time there arose the question of censorship. Alexander, keenly interested in political affairs, would avidly watch the news and listen to the radio. In the autumn of 1989 our house buzzed with an excitement that he shared, as the Berlin Wall fell and Eastern Europe was released from the grip of communist control that had compelled his grandfather, George Faludy, Hungary's national poet, to live in exile for over thirty years. On Christmas Day, Nikolai Ceausescu, the Romanian leader, was executed. Alexander knew as much as we did of the political corruption of the man, and could not understand why we turned off the television when pictures were about to be shown of Nikolai and Elena Ceausescu's death by a firing squad. Children see people being killed on television news on an almost daily basis, but there was something ghastly, pathetic and strangely personal about the execution of this tyrant which we thought could be emotionally damaging to one so young. Nevertheless, he deeply resented our refusal to let him see the pictures and would allude to the episode with a very real sense of grievance for a long time after.

This exemplifies one of the major problems for parents bringing up exceptionally intelligent children: there is a clear mismatch between intellectual, chronological and emotional development that has to be carefully handled so as not to cause offence. At the same time one must protect the sensitivity of the child.

During his second year there was still the expectation at school that it would be possible for Alexander to catch up. He was basically happy at this time, for his teacher clearly appreciated him and enjoyed his company. She recognised that Alexander was very eager to please, and tackled tasks set him with enthusiasm. She urged him to keep trying and not lose heart and commended his sense of humour and politeness.

Alexander's penultimate year in the pre-prep was a miserable one. The problems were that he did not fit into the norm of conventional behaviour shared by the other boys, and although he had no difficulty with the concepts concerned, his intelligence did not manifest itself in neatly presented work. His teacher recognised that Alexander had a vivid imagination, but that he had great difficulty translating this onto paper. When she could, the teacher would try out ways of helping, for example by writing down his answers and then giving them to him to copy. This kind of approach was helpful, not only in English, but in Mathematics, where it is impossible to get the right answer if you have copied down the numbers in the wrong columns, as was his practice.

We were grateful for this effort, but Alexander felt very much an outsider, and his answers, even if correct, were untidy. He had a strict moral code and wanted to do the right thing, but feared being branded as a tell-tale if he reported how the others treated him. He was consequently subjected to what seemed to him a vindictive and merciless ordeal of bullying from the other boys. Even if it blatantly occurred in front of his eyes, Andrew found it difficult to intervene because, as he now worked at the school, he had to maintain a clear distinction between his roles as teacher and parent. He did, however, bring up the matter at parents' evening, but was told that the mother of the boys in question had already protested that night because she was fed up with the complaints of others that her sons were picking on their children! To me this seemed that the implication was that we had said something improper, and were very much considered to be in the wrong for speaking out and drawing attention to our son's suffering.

After further consultations at school, it was agreed that it would be a good idea to pay for Alexander to have special remedial lessons twice a week during lunch time. A pleasant Scottish lady was found and the lessons began. However, after a few weeks she advised us that really the best thing to do would be to take Alexander out of such an academic institution and send him to a local state school where he would probably find his own level around the middle of the class.

We were unhappy with this suggestion, but not because of any objection to state schools: I was educated entirely in the state system, and in the days of the eleven plus, went to the local grammar school where I comfortably passed nine 'O' and three 'A' levels, and my mother is on the Governing Bodies of two local primary schools. We felt that Alexander had a keen intelligence which would thrive best in a self-consciously academic environment, if only his talents could somehow be accommodated. We were, in fact, so impressed with the school and its values that, after Alexander had been there for a while, Andrew had applied for, and accepted, a post teaching in the upper part of the school. The school has three sections: the pre-prep, four to eight; the lower school, eight to eleven, and the upper school eleven to eighteen. It was our fervent wish to maintain a continuity in Alexander's education so that he would remain there until he left at the age of eighteen.

Alexander's problems were not just restricted to the classroom: getting changed for games was another area where he became the butt of others' jokes. We had already adopted the expedient of buying him slip-on plimsolls and velcro-fastening school shoes, but that didn't help with the problem of his tie and the fiendishly awkward top button of his shirt. We practised for hours with the tie, until by repetition of 'round, one, two, up and through' he achieved a knot of sorts, but his top button defeated all our efforts. Here, his head teacher proved very helpful. She suggested that I remove the button, close up the hole, sew the 'dummy' button on top, and attach velcro to the actual fastening process. This cunning device proved invaluable and added another notch in our growing awareness that the way forward with Alexander was not to spend hours on inauthentic labour, but to find ways that would allow him to function to the best of his ability.

PE itself was a nightmare for Alexander. He couldn't catch balls and always, to the dismay of his team, missed them in football, and was hopeless on Sports' Day. I was used to his coming last, and expected no other outcome, but one year he was in the sack race. The starting pistol sounded, and little Emily and I stared in growing horror as all the others bounced off in a group. If it had been a running race, coming last wouldn't have been so bad, as no matter how slow one is, it does not take *that* long to get to the finishing line. My son, however, jumped, fell, shuffled and stumbled his way to the end in what seemed to us, and probably was for him, an eternity. Emily squeezed my hand.

'Oh, dear, mummy,' she chirped, 'brother (her pet name for him) was in a sack. He was hopping, and hopping, and hopping – he was wasting his time!'

We had been living, since just before Alexander's birth, in a solid, semi-detached, five bedroomed late-Victorian house in Southsea. Alexander initially occupied a 'suite' of rooms – or rather one large one that had been cunningly subdivided by the previous owners for letting purposes, into a big room, a tiny room and a small lobby. The large room was his play area, the small one his bedroom, and in the lobby stood a brightly painted chest of drawers topped with teddy bears. When I became pregnant with Emily, we moved his bed to the play room to accustom him to the transition to a 'big boy's' room thus preventing any resentment as the move was not connected in his mind with the baby's arrival. These rooms were delightful. As we hadn't had enough money to carpet the whole house, I went around all the carpet shops in Portsmouth buying up samples for about fifty pence each and created an exciting mosaic of good quality squares. The walls we painted white, with bright green skirtings. Air balloon light shades hung from the ceilings. I papered the walls with the children's greeting cards, from birth onwards, to create a sense of continuity and instil a feeling of how valued and loved they were. Different cards could be identified with particular people, some of whom would interestingly, whether consciously or not, pick out designs with recurring characteristics each year. For example, Gwen, an old friend of Andrew from his youth in Canada, would choose designs with multiple figures on – be they small, comic rabbits, or quaint, idiosyncratic trees.

While on the one hand this house represented space and security, we gradually became aware of a desire to move. We had, by Southsea standards, a long garden, but it was hemmed in on all sides by no fewer than nine properties, which backed on to and overlooked it. We felt that there was no privacy. A pub had recently re-opened at the end of the road, and the area became rough and rowdy at night time. Our cars, which were parked on the street, were broken into and vandalised with predictable regularity, the offences ranging in magnitude from the theft of small change from the glove compartment to smashed windows and a stolen battery.

I was telling a colleague about the latest horror – a trail of vomit over the front gate and rubbish thrown into the garden – when she mentioned how they had moved out of the city to the peaceful hill slopes overlooking it. She said that an old house around the corner from her was for sale. It had a curious history, in that a family with four children had moved into it seventy years previously and had stayed there until the siblings, all unmarried, had eventually died.

Andrew and I drove past it out of interest the following weekend – we liked the outside and fell in love with its character as soon as we walked through the door. The house had stood empty for two years, and was damp and dilapidated, but it was detached with a fine garden and many fruit trees; in the hall, next to a fine wooden staircase, remarkable stained glass was reflected in a massive, gilt framed old mirror. Carefully disguised under a layer of protective dirt, the delicate tendrils of an art nouveau design decorated brass door plates that begged to be polished. It didn't matter that it had fewer rooms than our current house – this home with a soul was the one for us.

The transition, however, was not a smooth one: we priced our house below the market value, found a buyer within a week, and moved in with my parents as a temporary measure whilst renovation took place. Repairs were extensive, the builders slow, and the four of us stayed with my mother and father (whose generosity at this difficult time made the whole transfer possible) cramped into their three bedroom house for seven months.

We thought it important that, although he was clearly different, Alexander should be given the opportunity to take part in as many activities as other children. At this time, he therefore joined the Beavers. He loved and took pride in the uniform and values of the pack, and the leadership was enthusiastic, firm and even-handed. During their weekly one hour session, the children were kept constantly busy, and there was, as a result, no opportunity for bullying here.

Uncomfortable with the mockery of his peers, Alexander tended to make friends with older people. One such person was Mrs Pawson, a breeder of Pyrennean Mountain dogs to whom I had been introduced at the age of fifteen, and I had visited at her isolated bungalow at Hambledon ever since. He became very attached to her and would groom her dogs and frolic in the orchard with them. Particularly exciting times were when puppies were born. Trusted and shoeless (to avoid spreading infection to the puppies before their injections) Alexander would sit in the warmth of the mother's birth nest, cuddling the blind pups as they misguidedly sucked his fingers. On occasions he would spend the night at Hambledon. The presence of fifteen, extremely large, white dogs obviated any anxiety about his safety in so remote a location.

As with all parts of his life, we felt there was no need to force Alexander into an ill-fitting conventionality, whether it was educational or social in nature. If wandering with a dog twice his size down a muddy path in a remote rural location likely to appeal to characters in a Thomas Hardy novel suited him better than playing football with his contemporaries, then we were content to let him be.

Alexander's Account:

As I sit here in my bedroom with my favourite pens in front of me and the tape recorder (borrowed from my sister as mine has again broken through over use), in an evening in late April which is supposed to be summer but proves merely to be a premature foretaste of autumn, or even an extension of it, lightened only by a few lonely buds on the trees, I find it rather difficult to talk about the events which occurred between 1988 and 1990, when I was between the ages of five and seven. This is not because these events are not clear in my mind, or that I am not able to recollect them at all, but because so much happened in that expanse of time.

The beginning of this period was marked by my entry into the pre-prep on the basis of an oral and visual examination when I was five years old. For some very strange reason, at that time I actually started to miss my old nursery school. I may not be able to account for it now, but I suppose the reason was a natural reaction to having to leave behind something to which I had become accustomed. This did not stay with me for long, as I found a new school to deal with and new people to meet challenging.

Within a few months of my arrival, two very important markers in my dyslexic case history emerged: the first, and most basic, was that my use of my left and right hands became more or less even, and in places, alternated, a fact that rather puzzled my class teacher. This led to one week of constant examination before school started, by another teacher, who was the first to put forward the suggestion that I might be dyslexic.

Of course I was oblivious to this definition at the time, and my parents didn't do anything about it – not because they didn't care, but because no-one we knew could give us enough information about dyslexia to help, and the teacher who carried out the test was not formally qualified to diagnose me as having the condition.

For any five year old to be confronted with new teachers in a new and confusing environment is a struggle, but to discover within the first couple of months of my arrival that I was somehow different, yet again, but for slightly other reasons, made things all the more troublesome. I encountered the same problems of not being liked because I was physically weak and uncoordinated.

However, the very fact that I had received this 'special' treatment was enough to throw me back into the isolation which had been a problem at my last school. It came gradually, and for quite a while I was happy there, and life seemed to continue in a nearly normal way for some time afterwards.

Normal? Well, not quite. Normal for me, but not normal as other people might view it. My contemporaries came round to the conclusion quite quickly, *that I wasn't one of them.* I wasn't any good at throwing a ball, reading, or beating someone up for no apparent reason.

This led to a reoccurrence of the bullying problem, but I don't think *they* thought of it as that, and at that age, cannot be deemed responsible for their actions; maybe they thought they were acting out a kindness by trying to make it clear to me what they were interested in. However, as I showed no apparent willingness to join in, they unconsciously isolated me. On the rare occasions when I felt I couldn't do anything else but join in, they rejected me.

This led me to turn back to my previous, and partially abandoned, hidden kingdom, where the grey of the castle walls was that in BBC cassettes, and the cement, uncoiled reels of tape – though not in the physical sense, I may add.

I made a strategic withdrawal into the realms of Tolkien, via cassettes of dramatisations of *Lord of the Rings* and *The Hobbit*, and later, an encyclopaedia of these works of fantasy. The world of Gorgoroth and Gondolin seemed to have a rather reassuring touch, as did the discovery that even though the good have to make sacrifices, the result, on the whole, is generally pleasing. The world of Gorgoroth and Gondolin seemed to be preferable to the classroom. It was in some ways painful to know that I wasn't like the others, but it also helped me to explore my intellectual capabilities and use my, by then, acknowledged memory to remember the intricacies of the plot and develop my skills. It gave me some consolation and hope for my own situation. My unique interest in these topics (by that I mean unique for my age), however, instead of helping me, seemed to isolate me more, since whenever I tried to talk to the other children about, say, *The Hitchhiker's Guide to the Galaxy*, they said, 'The hitchhiker's what?' and turned out not to be interested in the slightest.

My second year there brought me to a new class, and a teacher whom I liked, although I would like to add that my first one had also been very good. Here, with enjoyable lessons and stimulating material, I found myself consciously in the bizarre scenario, that, unlike most of the other pupils, I preferred the classroom to the playground. However, this dream-like state could not last for ever. Time goes on, and so do year group changes.

My entrance into the third year group coincided with my father's taking a place on the school staff. For some reason I hoped things would get better because of this, but in fact the reverse happened. Because my father was a member of the staff it made it difficult for him to complain. It's one thing if you're a parent and want to point something out: if you're a member of staff you have to be careful not to offend your colleagues.

Despite my then quite wide literary knowledge, ranging through Douglas Adams' *The Hitchiker's Guide to the Galaxy*, and J.R.R. Tolkien's *The Lord of the Rings*, I was no good at my English class, something that rather upset me. One of the main reasons for this was the fact that my spelling was bad, and my handwriting slow and abominable. It hurt to write, because I had to write so quickly to keep up. I was forcing myself against my natural capabilities to give myself reassurance that I could take down what the teacher had written on the board accurately. I would wait until she had finished writing it all out, by which time most people had already begun. My strategy worked against me because it took me much longer to finish, which incurred very harsh rebuffs, something that wounded me quite deeply. My limited academic achievement in both my Maths and my English class led this teacher to put forward the proposition that my qualities were incompatible with those which would be required in the next part of the school.

The turmoil of my academic career at that point was matched by my own personal sense of confusion: we were having to move house and stay with my grandparents at the same time. We were in constant disarray, and our minds were in three places: the place where we were, the place where we had been, and the place we were going to. So the sudden bombshell of my unsuitablity which was dropped on us made things impossible.

The school did provide limited help, which was rather humiliating for me. I was sent down in the period before lunch to the bottom class to be taught how to write letters properly – both joined up and printed – along with the five year olds, and I was also expected to go to lunch with this form, thus being reduced in my mind to the level of an incompetent. Ironically, along with humiliation, these lessons provided a brief relaxation of the situation in my normal class.

Later, my parents paid for a private tutor specialising in dyslexia to come and give me coaching. This meant I had to give up one of my lunchtimes each week. This was rather debilitating for me, since I was having to work all the time as well as being given extra work after school. The hour or so rest which I got at lunchtime was essential, and taking it away made things even worse for me.

Another way I tried to escape from the unpleasantness of my academic career was to go, as often as possible, to stay for the night at the house of a dog breeder friend of my parents. The friendship of people independent of my everyday existence, and the companionship of animals seemed to be preferable to that of my contemporaries who had decided that I deserved to be treated with a contempt (though I suppose they must not have thought of it as such) that one would show towards a repellent or alien animal.

CHAPTER THREE

A Testing Time

Having Alexander tested for dyslexia was very much on our minds, but there was the problem of finance. We were already paying for the two lessons a week, and the test would cost about another £130. We made inquiries which revealed that, theoretically, we could be put on a waiting list for a local authority assessment which might lead to a statement of special needs. As Alexander was not in a school run by the local authority, however, it would not be able to give him the support indicated in the statement and therefore it would be inappropriate to carry out an assessment if it couldn't lead to extra help being provided.

Our thoughts then turned to BUPA. We had been members since Alexander's birth, for, as we reasoned, although it was expensive, it was something that we felt, in our balancing of the budget, that we could not afford to be without in case something happened that required treatment not readily available through the NHS. We consulted our doctor to see if she could help us with referral to BUPA for assistance with assessment and tuition. She wrote a letter indicating that Alexander was an intelligent boy who was falling behind his peers because of what was suspected to be dyslexia and that in her opinion it would have a serious effect on his mental and emotional development if things were allowed to continue unchanged. We applied to BUPA who rejected our application for help. We resigned ourselves to further economies to fund his needs independently.

As the educational year drew to a close, discussions were held about Alexander's future in the school. It was mooted that the Lower School might not be the best place for him and that perhaps it would be a good idea if we began to investigate other options. These suggestions rang alarm bells in us, and being aware that Alexander had reached the recommended age for the dyslexic test, we booked an appointment for 27 July 1990.

Emily stayed with my parents, and it was with great trepidation that we drove Alexander to meet the educational psychologist, Mr Robin Freeland. We knew that our son had what we thought to be the symptoms of dyslexia, but all the same, we were worried about the implications of a psychological test. What would the psychologist find out? Would it have been better not to have known? Would the results in some way gain a hold on, and control, our lives?

Mr Freeland, a lively and outgoing man, greeted us, and explained the structure of the morning: he would test Alexander for about an hour while we went shopping or sat in the waiting room. He would then discuss his initial findings with us while Alexander completed some written work, and we would receive a comprehensive report in the post a few weeks later.

Too nervous to contemplate browsing around the shops, Andrew and I made desultory attempts at reading the novels we had brought with us, but abandoned them to engage in a fragmented discussion of deliberately unrelated matters. An eon later, Mr Freeland seemed to burst into the room, with news that was indeed to change the path of Alexander's life – yes, he was dyslexic, but his IQ of 135 on the WISC scale put him in the top one per cent of the population. His enthusiasm and enjoyment of the interview with Alexander was obvious when he laughingly reported that when he'd asked our son what areas of learning presented difficulty, the seven-year-old, instead of listing the normal concerns like copying from the board, had replied that some of the vocabulary in *Jane Eyre* was causing him problems. He also reported that he had had an insight into Alexander's condition before the test had even begun, when he had told him to go up the stairs and turn right. He had gone left instead!

Mr Freeland then explained the implications of his findings in detail. The gap of 30 points between his verbal and non-verbal IQ scores gave a clear indication of the nature of his dyslexic difficulties. He was found to be extremely articulate, scoring almost at the top of the scale in the comprehension sub-test, while abstract reasoning and acquisition of vocabulary were at a very superior level. In contrast, there was a dramatic weakness in the coding sub-test, which was seen as an indication of a problem in hand–eye coordination and short term visual memory. Tests pursuing his visual recall indicated that Alexander found it hard to hold information in his visual store, and this would have implications for copying from the blackboard and committing visual information to his long term store, such as learning the spelling of new words.

In fine motor tasks Alexander had been given eight basic letter shapes to copy, but here he had been unable even to reproduce the vertical lines with any degree of accuracy. His sequencing of common patterns revealed uncertainty in reciting the alphabet, and major omissions in the months of the year. This was in contrast to his remarkably good long term memory which had always enabled him to repeat complete stories which he had heard on tape.

Andrew and I tried to take notes during this discussion, but found the totality of information hard to grasp. For, all at once, there were special reasons and explanations for the particular oddities and inconsistencies in Alexander's achievements. Mr Freeland reiterated that all these details and more would be contained in the written report and went on to outline his recommendations. The most basic, and easily fulfilled, was the purchase of pen grips to encourage a conventional grasp. Referral to an occupational therapist was suggested to help with his motor difficulties. The reversal problems in his writing were seen as indicators of quite serious visual impairment and we were advised to visit a specialist orthoptist.

Word processing skills were seen as important, not only to encourage Alexander's ability to communicate on paper, but also to forestall some of the frustrations a pupil of his calibre would inevitably experience when grappling with pen, paper and ideas. In recognition of his inherent difficulty with writing, Mr Freeland thought that at school Alexander should be given every opportunity to shine orally through means of presentation other than the written word.

Two sessions a week of multi-sensory learning with a specialist were suggested, as was the technique of paired reading – something we could do for ten minutes a night with him. All this advice seemed both perplexing in the magnitude of its scope and essential if we were to free Alexander from his fetters, but the thing which most stuck in my mind, and which actually altered the course of his life, was Mr Freeland's statement that a child as intelligent as our son could easily become frustrated and develop all sorts of anti-social behavioural problems if we did not find some way of satisfying his potential. I determined during that interview that such a bleak outlook would not be the fate of my son, and that I would personally see to it that he would be fulfilled.

The journey home was in marked contrast to the one there. Our son with the illegible writing and bizarre spelling was both dyslexic and one of the cleverest people in the country. Alexander was buoyant as he chatted about his interesting conversation with Mr Freeland. He was liberated from the labels of slow, backward, stupid, and the basis of a new aspect of his character was formed: an independence from relying on the conventional judgements of others and an awareness that his individuality had a unique quality which was outside standard measurements. That morning he ceased to mind being different and gained a new strength in the belief of his personal worth.

I had a strong sense that we had reached some sort of pivotal point with the information we had received. Alexander clearly had great potential and if we could only find a way of giving it a means of expression, we could rescue him from the prospect of underachievement that had been painted at the conference on dyslexia I had attended a couple of years before.

Then the idea came to me that if Alexander was in the top one per cent of the population, then perhaps he was clever enough to join MENSA. Andrew was not enthusiastic, to put it mildly.

'Dyslexics wouldn't stand a chance with their tests,' he said. 'We'd be wasting our time. It's not worth trying. Forget it!'

I wouldn't let the matter drop. What had become clear to me was that, ironically, if Alexander was to be recognised in his own right, we had to have external verification of his intellect in terms that would be universally recognised. I rang MENSA and told them his score on the WISC test, and to my amazement they said that on their more commonly recognised scale, his IQ would actually be 154! They also explained that there were two ways of entry into MENSA – either scoring high enough on their test or by submitting an independent psychologist's report for their review. I had to resign myself to a long wait, for we wouldn't get the written test results for about a month, and then we would have to await MENSA's scrutiny of its findings.

We decided not to tell anyone (apart from my parents) about the possibility of MENSA membership as I have always been a firm believer in not publicly counting my chickens before they have hatched. I knew, however, that I was on the right track, for to say 'my child is dyslexic but really very clever' is to invite condescending acquiescence, but to say 'my child is a member of MENSA' is an absolute statement and cannot be derided.

Alexander's final year in the pre-prep began and we gave his new teacher (who was head of this section of the school) a copy of the report. This year marked the introduction of girls into the school, a move generally welcomed by many for their civilising effect upon the boys, and opposed by the traditionalists. Alexander formed a close friendship with a little girl in the year below his and throughout that academic year they were inseparable.

The school's stance was still that we should consider other options for the next autumn so, accordingly, we visited a delightful five to sixteen private day school in the middle of the rolling wooded hills of the Hampshire countryside. This establishment recognised the prevalence of, and the specific needs related to, dyslexia: there was a unit to which children

were withdrawn on a regular basis for tuition with a specialist teacher. We were made welcome here and the headmistress was very interested in Alexander's report. The school
was small, with a personal touch and in many ways it seemed
ideal, for here was somewhere that would recognise his
intellectual strengths while catering for his dyslexic difficulties. We discussed the matter at length, but in the end our
reservation prevailed, for at that time we still thought that
school was the place to provide Alexander with his education, and this one, delightful as it was, seemed to lack the
intellectual cutting edge of the one he at present attended
and which we considered his mind best suited to.

The problem now was how to convince the school that
he should be allowed to stay: a solution presented itself in
October when MENSA rang to say that it had accepted him.
I telephoned our local newspaper which immediately indicated a wish to do an article on Alexander. A photographer
and reporter met us at the school and searched for suitable
locations to photograph him. His class teacher was initially
present, and I felt rather deflated when she told the reporter
that it was a pity that others in the class hadn't tried for
MENSA for they were just as intelligent. Alexander noticed
nothing, however, and in the end he was photographed on
an elegant carved step ladder in the library with a volume
of Thomas Hardy's poetry open in his lap; this was entirely
appropriate, for even though the book would not be his
chosen means of access to the poems, he was certainly
familiar with their contents on tape.

During the interview itself I did not mention the fact of
Alexander's dyslexia, not because I was ashamed, but because he had suffered from it so much that I felt it was about

time that he was given some credit purely for his intellect. This was not to be my practice in future years, but I felt that it was important for his self-esteem then.

The article was published hours before the school's open evening. There was a small colour picture on the front page of the newspaper, captioned 'Boy Wonder' and a larger black and white picture with the article on an inside page. The school librarian cut out the material and put it on display. In the festival atmosphere of the open evening Alexander glowed with pride as people came up and congratulated him, and his classmates, some of whom had previously shunned him, gathered round, now glad of the association. Although Alexander was not fooled by this fleeting camaraderie, the whole episode reinforced his sense of personal worth, and the growing belief that he did not have to be like the rest.

The next day Andrew met Alexander's teacher in the quadrangle – the head teacher who had expressed doubts on his second day at the school. This time she told him that it was ridiculous that Alexander should be photographed with a book that he could not read. My husband retorted that our son knew many of the poems by heart and understood them. We had clearly won a battle, but not the war: however, there was no more talk of him having to leave the school.

At Beavers that week, the leader congratulated him in front of the pack but, unfortunately, as with earlier experiences with his stories at school, asked him to read the article to the other boys. Of course he could not, with any degree of fluency or accuracy, and felt rather silly, and even fraudulent about his achievement. This was so typical of the problems we have had with people's lack of comprehension of the actual functional nature of his condition. We had explained his difficulties when he joined but there was nothing malicious in the leader's intent: indeed, she had been trying to make him feel good without realising that the way to achieve this would have been to read the article for him.

We eventually moved into our new house late in October 1990. Alexander and Emily loved the roaring fires which burned in the living room grate on cold autumn evenings and enjoyed scouring the garden for twigs to dry for tinder. They seemed to think that they had arrived in a new world with its own special customs and traditions.

As with my initial purchase of the tapes, Alexander's Christmas present that year was not premeditated. During the period of renovation, we had had to arrange the restoration of the art nouveau stained glass in our hall way. The two women who completed the task were very skilful, and as all the windows in the house had to be replaced anyway, we had also commissioned some original designs from them. The fanlights to the 1930s bay extension to the dining room merited the installation of a truly spectacular deco sunburst. In the bathroom, the cracked Edwardian suite had to be removed, but we were particularly attached to the wrought iron toilet cistern which was embossed with the cryptic legend *The Avenue*. So, instead of going for discreet, opaque glass in the window, Melissa Vogel designed us a panel with purple words *The Avenue* running diagonally from bottom left to top right, encroached upon by fecund, entwining leaves that stylistically can only be described as feeling like a strange combination of of art nouveau and can-can! In Emily's room, her name appeared in the fan lights, flanked by roses reflecting her middle name.

We wanted to do something special for Alexander, so we consulted with our experts about producing a large window based on themes and characters in *The Lord of the Rings* with Gandalf featuring large. It turned out to be impractical to design it as an actual window, for as his room had sashes, he wouldn't be able to see out if it was incorporated in one of the panes. We settled on a splendid, back-lit wood framed design that would hang above his mantelpiece.

I was due to collect this masterpiece a few weeks before Christmas, but to my horror I received a phone call saying that they had lost the use of their workshop and would not be able to complete the order.

I therefore had to think of another present fast, and on the spur of the moment bought him a stereo radio cassette player. This last minute substitution proved a godsend. Alexander, although he still loved his tapes, became an avid radio listener, starting with the the new Radio Five and progressing to Radio Four, which has become like a friend to him, and is a source of a large part of his knowledge. He loves the radio, and listens to news, current affairs, plays, discussions, satires, educational programmes and, for an hour each Sunday morning, *The Archers*.

The test had made so many recommendations that it was hard to know where, apart from pen grips, to start. We thought we'd try the Occupational Therapist and had to visit our doctor, to whom we had sent a copy of the report, for referral. The assessment took place on 23rd October during half-term and largely served the useful purpose of quantifying the awkwardness and clumsiness, of which we had become progressively aware since he had been a few months old, into a form which could be readily assimilated by others.

His balance was found to be poor with an excessive use of his flailing arms and a difficulty in remaining in one place when asked to stand on one leg. When trying to catch a ball, Alexander held his arms wide with palms upwards and did not move to intercept it when it was aimed slightly out of reach. He managed to kick a stationary ball although he tended to overbalance and be too vigorous in his kicking stroke. A moving ball was a different matter, however, as he had difficulty with the timing and could not control the power or speed.

When asked to copy a circle, Alexander drew it clockwise, and started a square from the bottom. He had problems when tackling a triangle and had to have several attempts at copying a diamond before he produced a shape that could be recognised.

Alexander's visual memory was found to be poor: he was only able to remember three out of seven objects and, interestingly, could not name them directly, instead describing them in terms of their properties.

The Occupational Therapist strongly advised that Alexander attend group therapy sessions: as these were held in school time, this proved an unpopular course of action. Instead, we were given tasks to undertake with him at home. There were exercises: with putty and pegs to develop his fingers as he had displayed diminished strength in both hands; with balls, rolled, tossed, dropped, bounced, struck, lobbed and caught in a variety of positions to improve his body awareness, laterality and coordination.

The Occupational Therapist also paid several visits to the school to make recommendations in consultation with his teacher as to practices that would help him in class. Her other recommendations included assessment by a speech therapist, for a closer look at his language, and by a local educational psychologist with a view to a statement of extra help required in the classroom. She agreed with Mr Freeland's suggestion of Alexander learning to use a word processor and thought that the use of a tape recorder in the classroom situation was a possibility that needed to be investigated. One of her most helpful contributions was to provide us with the name of an orthoptist specialising in dealing with children whose problems were similar to Alexander's. There seemed to be so much to do that we were not able to take on board all the recommendations at once, because we found each successive report had a domino effect. Andrew spent hours doing the exercises with Alexander.

By Christmas, Alexander's report, in conventional terms, had not improved. His teacher commented that his hand-writing and spelling were a nightmare and, as he had to think hard about every word, he was slow and could not finish on time. She found the content of his work interesting and noted that he could remember spelling rules, which was of course in marked contrast to his inability to spell on paper.

Alexander still enjoyed writing and dictating things to me – these had by now left the realm of stories and become his thoughts about life and man's role in relation to God, the world and moral and spiritual culpability. After a few weeks down this path of soul searching on behalf of human-ity and towards the end of his seventh year, he started writing poetry. These oral compositions did not have regular verse forms, but were concentrated thoughts and feelings which I think can be considered as poetry. There were many poems, but I have selected my favourites in the Appendix. The first he wrote was *The Slumbers of the Sleeping Stars*. As he wandered around dictating it to me, I was moved as the words forming shapes on the paper gave me an insight into his mind and its capacity for appreciating the complex beauty of simple objects. The stars became synaethesised as he talked of their singing, shining and dancing. The boundaries between his mind and the heavens merged as their activities took place both in the medium of observer and observed. The 'knowl-edge' of the stars was both his knowledge of them and the wisdom they contained. I felt humble that a child could look at the stars and feel 'joy' – an emotion pure and uncorrupted. The whole was a description of falling asleep – it was so typically Alexander – novels were things he'd *heard*, not read, and at night, similarly, he listened to the stars.

Some poems were to us strangely reminiscent of the ideas which interested his Hungarian grandfather. In *The End of All Ends*, he adopted as declamatory a tone as could be expected of a child envisaging the destruction of man and the world through man's industrial greed: 'As Electricity plants work their horrid engines'. The anger reminded me of a verse from his grandfather's *Learn by Heart this Poem of Mine*, translated into English by Robin Skelton in 1980:

> Learn by heart this poem of mine;
> recite it when the putrid tides
> that stink of lye break from their beds,
> when industry's rank vomit spreads
> and covers every patch of ground,
> when they've killed every lake and pond,
> Destruction humped upon its crutch,
> black rotting leaves on every branch;
> when gargling plague chokes Springtime's throat
> and twilight's breeze is poison, put
> your rubber gas mask on and line
> by line declaim this poem of mine.

One of his grandfather's particular interests is Platonism, and although Alexander knew nothing of this at that time, I speculated if there could be some sort of genetic memory that could enable a child who had just turned eight to write in *Poetry Itself* of the nature of poetry in terms of 'form' and celebrating

this
Glorious pattern
of
feelings.

His desire to write poetry spanned a period of about six months from January to June 1991. At school the term's topic had been the study of Greek myths and legends. Alexander was absent for a couple of days while he recovered from the effects of swallowing too much water during an after school swimming lesson, so he decided to write his teacher a poem, *The Imprisonment of Persephone*. I was impressed with his developing ability to manipulate language and create atmosphere in a description of physical and mental deprivation:

Tortured with hunger and withered in soul.

Two years were to pass before Alexander again asked me to write down one of his poems for him.

During the period he was composing poetry, we made a few attempts to see if it could be published – *The Birds* was sent to a BBC *Blue Peter* competition about animals. It didn't get an entry into the book which was published as a result of material received, but in retrospect I suppose it didn't fit in with conventional expectations.

Having by chance seen a translation of one of Andrew's father's poems in *Outposts*, we sent some examples of Alexander's work to the editor, but as far as I remember his reply, he explained that Alexander was too young to have developed any technical skills that could enable his work to be considered as poetry. It wasn't until he was nine that the form of his work was to match the quality of its content – but that's another story.

Alexander's Account:

Although there was great suspicion that I had dyslexia, there was no official confirmation until the summer of 1990 at the time when we were staying with my grandparents while our house was being renovated. My parents made an appointment with a specialist.

I remember going round and round the roundabout in the centre of the nearby town as we tried to work out which way to turn, finally parking a short distance from the building itself. Our confusion stuck in my mind and was perhaps symbolic of the lack of direction in my life at this point.

For the session I was taken upstairs alone by the specialist and shown into a small room. There was a broad brown wood table and two chairs. I sat opposite him and was asked a number of questions read from a sheet. I remember one in particular because I found some difficulty in answering it. It was, rather surprisingly, 'what is the purpose of parliament?' My immediate inclination at that age was to answer 'to make stupid arguments all day long', but I knew that this would not have been appropriate so, I sat there for about two minutes thinking it through and eventually came up with the only answer I could: 'to pass laws, I think'. I was also asked a number of questions about what I found difficult. The queerest answer that I gave was relating to the vocabulary in *Jane Eyre*. He seemed rather surprised at this and then asked me in detail about what I liked and disliked in the book. His puzzlement grew, I remember, when I started quoting the opening passage. He then commented on the fact that he also liked it and asked me how I had managed to memorise it.

On the way back my parents told me that I was indeed dyslexic and that I was also 'a very clever frog' (my father's nickname for me). I was told to keep quiet about it, and that my teacher would know, and that would be it, and that they were very pleased with me.

In my last year in the pre-prep, I moved to a new class, that of the headmistress. This is what I had originally hoped for, after being told by a boy of the last year group in the preceding term that although the head was strict, the best behaved children were sent into her class, and that the less well behaved ones, or as he put it, 'the naughty ones' got put into the other top class, that of an equally nice teacher, less strict (a claim refuted by the staff).

So I entered my last year with a mixed sense of fear and achievement. However, the sense of achievement was not to last for long, as I was put into the semi-official bottom maths set. Also, partly I feel to satisfy what I saw as *the school's desire to have me thrown out,* and partly as an attempt by my parents to find me the best help possible, we went to have a look at a nearby day school. As with most children, I had a sentimental attachment to my own school. Also, I did not realise the full implications of the situation, and I was not fully informed of it – a kind thought by my parents who didn't want me to be worried. Even though I was quite impressed by what I saw, I didn't like the idea of moving.

Another important thing that occurred was the start of the school's attempt to try and make me do well at sport, something which, as I hope to show, is totally impossible. This first of all took the form of good natured extra swimming lessons after school with a group of other no hopers in the lower school swimming pool. From one perspective, this proved extremely good for me, to begin with at least, when I 'swam' my first width. However, this was a mixed blessing since I was off school for two days, vomiting after swallowing too much swimming pool water after going under so many times. I subsisted mainly on toast and tea plus a few biscuits, being unable to stomach (please excuse the pun) anything else.

During my first term in my last year in the pre-prep we moved from my grandparents' house (a stay forecast for two months which somehow turned into over half a year owing to problems with the building work) into our own home on the verge of the city, roughly five miles from its centre and a few minutes' drive from my grandparents. Here, I started to broaden my creativity and to write poetry which seems somewhat naive now but my parents thought to be extremely good for my age.

I saw poetry as something which took real intellectual stamina and determination, for, unlike prose, it is a sort of code or hidden language which only those sharing the poet's enthusiasm can unlock and have access to.

I found the actual selecting of words and the fitting of those words to a coherent meaning outside my imagination difficult, because we all attach our own meanings to what we say which others may not at first, or ever, grasp. So, it is necessary either to elaborate or to simplify, and that choice itself is difficult. But the method of implementing these decisions is even harder and that's what made poetry a challenge – one has to hold the attention of another human being, but at the same time convey one's meaning.

Poetry in its purest form is a complex analysis and interpretation of human behaviour and thought – its subject matter being what appeals to the human mind. This applies to the greatest poets – look at Milton when he wrote *Paradise Lost* – it's not just the story of the Fall from Grace or that of the angels – it's satisfying a human curiosity about what cannot be found in traditional scripture.

Poetry is not the mind on paper, for human thoughts have no actual existence in their raw form – they're just signals which pass through the brain. They can only acquire meaning to us if we impose an independent identity on them – generated through our philosophical analysis and influenced by the environment we have been brought into and the nature of language. Language is merely the transfer into external communication from the brain via the mouth: it is the manifestation of thought into a communicable form.

To understand the nature of things we first have to know what a thought looks like. Does a thought have a physical existence? Scientists have shown them as electronic beeps, but is that their real nature? Are they mere signals? Signals themselves have no meaning: they have to represent something else. So what do these impulses represent and how do they operate?

I know that what I have said appears to wander from the original track of an autobiography, but to understand the thinking behind poetry it's necessary to see why and how it happened.

+++++

I remember my first night in the house, gazing at my fire place, at that time not boarded up, and thinking the house to be haunted, a natural feeling in a new environment for most children; but this fear did not last for long, and things became very happy for me at home, especially at my first Christmas in the house, the December of 1990 when my parents got me a radio cassette player. For the first time I really listened to the radio, and I became somewhat addicted to Radio 5, especially to the children's programmes. This opened up a different world for me – not just the world of the cassette, which I knew off by heart, but a world of uncertainties, but which were generally pleasing. I couldn't memorise the programmes, since I only ever heard them once, but I could always remember the sort of things that had been said, and thought them over for a long, long time afterwards. I also imagined possible outcomes to stories which I'd heard on it which I made up myself.

This branch-out mentally coincided with the fear which many people of my age group, myself included, had of going to the next part of the school because of rumours spread about it, and about particular teachers in it, by a certain member of my year group. I wasn't sure whether to side with my contemporaries, or to look forward to it in earnest. The headmaster, whom at that time I liked, came to the pre-prep often during the last couple of terms to assess us for the lower school, although he said it wasn't a real examination. I seemed to feel a sort of equilibrium between my own apprehensions and the shared concerns with my contemporaries. I finally decided to look forward to it come what may until my last day of term in the summer when I remember saying at midday, which was the official end of school, to a contemporary, 'We're in the lower school now'. But I didn't actually feel I was in the lower school, or the pre-prep, and this I found rather terrifying. I realised that I could never go back fully to the old pre-prep and carry on the almost pleasurable existence which I had been leading there, but also that I had to go forward. I thought that the lower school would give me this opportunity to advance in the way in which I had been advancing in my own personal world and that they would welcome me and my studies with the same enthusiasm that my parents had, and that also they would be a little more impressed than the pre-prep by my acceptance into MENSA. Suddenly I had expectations of a new and different academic life.

Alexander, aged six months, with Granny and Grandad (George and Eileen) Spencer

The authors with George Faludy

Alexander, aged five-and-a-half years, with Andrew

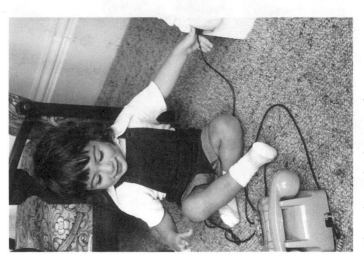

Alexander aged eighteen months

Alexander aged four years

Alexander, aged nine-and-a-half years, with Clifford Phillips

Alexander, aged ten-and-a-half years, in Budapest

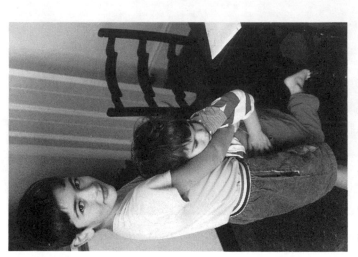

Alexander, aged six years, with Emily, aged two

Alexander, aged ten-and-a-half years, in Hungary with George Faludy

Alexander, aged twelve-and-a-half years, with Dr Dean and Emily in Petworth Park, August 1995

Alexander, aged eleven years (reproduced from The News, August 18th 1994)

Alexander's first visit to Milton Abbey in Autmn 1994, aged eleven years

CHAPTER FOUR

Education, not Schooling

'I never let my schooling interfere with my education.'
(Mark Twain)

I often wonder how different Alexander's life would be if it wasn't for my love of bargains. One day while browsing in Chichester in a book shop that dealt largely in remaindered stock, I came across a display of boxed BBC audio tapes and cartoon book versions of Shakespeare's *Othello*. The book contained the entire text, unabridged and unexpurgated but in a cartoon form with speech bubbles from marvellously animated and colourful characters. At £5 a set I thought it represented terrific value and I bought one on the off-chance that the book would come up on the 'A' level syllabus and I could educate and entertain my class at the same time.

The box – about half an inch thick and the size of a LP sat on a shelf for months. Then, in June 1991 Alexander noticed its eye-catching cover and asked if he could borrow it. Andrew and I exchanged amused glances as we assented – thoroughly expecting him to return it in a few minutes when he found the cartoons rather different from those in Dennis the Menace.

We heard the tape recorder being switched on in his bedroom and the pages of the book being turned. This was before we began carpeting the house and every sound in the upstairs rooms could be heard with irritating precision below.

To our amazement he did not emerge from his room for three whole hours. When he did join us, he was animated in a way I had never observed in him before. He talked about treachery, love, deceit, abuse of friendship and trust. His mind had been introduced to a new and exciting world of rich language, imagery and ideas. He loved it. There were awkward questions, too, such as 'Mummy, what's a courtesan?'

After he had eventually gone to bed Andrew and I marvelled at the capacity of his mind, not only in its comprehension of the text, but also the genuine excitement he felt at his introduction to Shakespeare. We wished that we had been able to record what he had said when it was fresh and inspired. The next best thing would be to ask him to talk about the play the following day and tape his response. Unfortunately, this plan failed because for some bizarre reason Emily's simple cassette player which I used managed to pick up radio signals instead.

I was afraid that Alexander would lose his enthusiasm and cutting edge if I merely asked him to talk about the book again, so this time I gave him an essay title, 'Trust in *Othello*' and asked him to talk about this theme. He began: '*Othello* is a fine example of the dangers of trust. It is displayed in several ways. One of them is the trust in Iago from Othello, who tricks him into thinking that Cassio is in love with his wife. The trust in Iago is a mislaid one...'

I was pleased how eagerly he packed in and analysed example after example and concluded that, 'this play of

Shakespeare has taught me not to trust so easily,' for a person's adopted image can be very different from his festering intent.

That night Andrew typed up Alexander's response. As experienced teachers, we were convinced that the essay was of GCSE standard but an unbiased independent opinion was needed. So Andrew asked a colleague, Robert Lister, to put a grade on it as a piece of GCSE course work, but he didn't tell him at this stage that eight-year-old Alexander was the author.

'There's something funny about this essay,' Robert remarked when he returned it to Andrew. 'It should be a grade A, but it isn't quite. There's something peculiar about the way it's expressed that I can't put my finger on!'

He had given it seventeen out of twenty – a top grade B – and commented: 'An essay showing a lively personal involvement in the play. The occasional awkwardness of style can be excused by the evident originality of the response.'

Robert's analysis was spot on. Alexander's oral style, which we had transcribed verbatim, would naturally seem puzzling to one unfamiliar with its method of composition. His response being untaught, was certainly completely original. Robert wanted to know the story behind the essay and when Andrew told him, he was suitably impressed – gratifyingly dumbfounded, in fact.

To Andrew and me the course ahead for Alexander was now clear. He was eight; he was still in the pre-prep; he could do GCSE. All we would have to do would be to give him a text to listen to every few weeks, an essay title and record his response. It would be like a game for him – an amusement. We thought it best not to tell him at this stage what he was actually doing in case in some way it spoiled his enjoyment. We also decided not to teach him at all at this level, for we did not want to interfere with his intuitive appreciation.

In the choice of texts, it has always been my policy with Alexander not go for the simple ones. I actually think it is harder to find enough of quality to say about a text which is not challenging. In any case, I wanted to educate Alexander and give him a true foundation in English Literature, rather than just making it easy for him to pass an examination.

Consequently the next task I set him, in July 1991, was a critical appreciation of *Care-Charmer Sleep* by the sixteenth century poet Samuel Daniel:

> Care-Charmer sleep, son of the sable night,
> Brother to death, in silent darkness born,
> Relieve my languish, and restore the light,
> With dark forgetting of my care's return.
> And let the day be time enough to mourn
> The shipwreck of my ill adventured youth;
> Let waking eyes suffice to wail their scorn,
> Without the torment of the night's untruth.
> Cease, dreams, the images of day-desires,
> To model forth the passions of the morrow;
> Never let rising sun approve you liars,
> To add more grief to aggravate my sorrow.
> > Still let me sleep, embracing clouds in vain;
> > And never wake to feel the day's disdain.

I read him the poem a couple of times and asked him to give his opinion of what it was all about. When transcribing his verbal responses or essays from tape we were careful always to give exact verbatim renderings. His work therefore truly represented a mind in action as Alexander thought his way into the the subject. It is an oral, not a written style, as can be seen in the opening two paragraphs of his essay:

> 'What Daniel is trying to explain to us is that sleep is a resort beyond resorts, a time for resting and to imagine what the next day will be like, though he describes it – he describes sleep and dreams as being liars.
>
> They are liars because they make images that are not true and the next day reality proves them wrong. Daniel calls these fantasies to stop...'

Alexander, although having no experience of death in the family, was able to appreciate Daniel's linking of it with sleep, or, to put it in his own words: 'Although related to death in this poem, sleep gently beckons the soul in to forget about the cares of the day.'

I was delighted with his intellectual development, but wanted to ensure that there were plenty of other aspects to his life. I thought it was about time, now that we had plenty of space, to buy the children pets. Mrs Pawson, the breeder of Pyrennean mountain dogs mentioned that after a fox had killed her two Aylesbury ducks she was going to buy some Khaki Campbells. She had had this breed of duck as a child and said they were very friendly.

As she clearly knew what she was doing, I asked her to order two for us and we agreed to collect them from her when they arrived. We had a month in which to get their accommodation ready. At the bottom of the garden is an old shed and an adjacent brick and wood structure that used to be a greenhouse when there was glass in the windows. Andrew covered the frame in chicken wire and we hauled in from the shed an old sideboard that he had purchased for

£5 in a junk shop in Brighton when he had been a student. We also bought a great roll of chicken wire and some bamboo poles to create a moveable pen for them to have on the lawn.

The curious little creatures arrived that summer and were the focus of the children's holiday. Emily called her duck Rose and Alexander named his Mabel. At first they had no wings – just stumps. I was quite relieved, as I have always been rather frightened by the idea of a bird flapping its wings when handled. Consequently, as their wings grew, I was totally familiar with Rose and Mabel as individuals and was not disturbed by their feathers at all.

At first the ducks did not like being touched, but one afternoon Emily spent hours chasing them round the garden. The birds eventually gave up, sat down, and let themselves be handled – she had tamed them. From that day on they were truly pets. They would come when called, sit on our laps, coo, and march up to the back door to demand bread. They tried to come in but I drew the line at having them in the house. My favourite photographs of that summer are of Rose and Mabel splashing in the paddling pool with the children.

Andrew had made it his special task to help Alexander to follow the exercise programme that had been recommended by the Occupational Therapist, Mrs Annette Urry, but there were other recommendations that were harder to pursue. Mrs Urry had been most helpful when I had inquired how to find an orthoptist specialising in problems such as Alexander's. She contacted the local orthoptist service who suggested a Mrs Fowler at the Royal Berkshire Hospital at Reading. When I contacted the hospital, I was told that we were out of the area and couldn't be seen.

However, after protracted negotiations and a referral from our doctor we eventually got an appointment in July 1991. Alexander was wired up to strange machines and every aspect of his vision was monitored: the results were a revelation. Apart from being, as we knew, myopic, his main visual problem became obvious on recording his eye movements with infra red recorders to foveal targets. He was found to have great difficulty in keeping his eyes quite still and in making accurate and saccadic and pursuit movement. Mrs Fowler thought that this difficulty with his eyes may well have caused letters to move about and mirror-reverse.

I was astounded by the implications of her discovery. It explained so much. Reality was constantly shifting for Alexander, and even if the dyslexia was not purely a visual problem, Mrs Fowler's observations certainly threw a light on his clumsiness.

Alexander was given complicated eye exercises to complete on a regular basis: they were based on the principle of physiological diplopia. This apparently means that if someone looks at an object, and then holds a second object in front or behind the first, the second object will appear double. This phenomenon is only possible if the eyes are working together as a pair.

We found the instructions very hard to follow and weren't really certain that we could do the exercises properly ourselves, let alone monitor that Alexander was doing them correctly, for how can you judge what someone else is seeing? Nevertheless, we added the eye exercises to the daily round suggested by Mrs Urry.

The autumn term loomed ominously ahead, for such rumours of the barbarity of the lower school had filtered into the pre-prep through older brothers, perhaps harbouring malicious intent, that many pre-prep pupils were genuinely traumatised at the thought of leaving the security of their first school environment. New uniforms had to be purchased, not just for Alexander but for Emily, who at four and a half was joining the pre-prep. I think Alexander reached a sort of mental equilibrium between excitement at a new beginning and a slight unease in case the gossip about the place was true.

He was particularly interested in religion, and thoroughly enjoyed church parade with the cubs, to which he had progressed. Conversations about theological issues such as the nature of free will and predestination were favourites then. So we explained to him about the concept of original sin and its permeation of the thought processes of writers in previous centuries. He was keen to look at some more poems, so I thought this was a good time to introduce him to John Donne's *A Hymn to God the Father*.

Alexander enjoyed unravelling the thoughts in the poem as he verbally felt his way into it. His style is unorthodox: it reflects the bizarre excitement of an eight-year-old grappling with complex ideas:

> '...he committed a sin by teaching others to sin and he "made my sin their door"; he was their door to becoming sinful and deceitful – he was the teacher of sin by which he committed sin himself. By saying he was their door to sin he was saying that he was their portal to wickedness.'

By the autumn, optimism had replaced trepidation in Alexander. The children posed eagerly for their beginning of the school year photographs in the back garden. It was a new start for them both, and the photo another of those rites of passage rituals that mark the stages in growing up.

Alexander felt quite positive after his first day for, as many new children joined at this stage, he was for the first time not an outsider. We, too, felt fairly confident about his future in the school as we had taken the precaution of meeting Alexander's new headmaster and discussing the dyslexic report so that staff could be informed of his problems.

As the term got underway, hideous complications began to rear their heads. Alexander was miserable and frustrated: he had to give up cubs because he could not keep pace with the homework. He was impeccably behaved at school where he was unable to achieve, so his anger boiled over at home in the face of tasks which, for a dyslexic child, had no educational value. These included copying out material at home which he had not been able to complete in class. At the extreme, this involved a frightful maximum of four hours one night as Alexander became progressively more confused copying a piece of science which he had incorrectly transcribed by starting in the wrong place. When his teacher found out what he had done, he tore the offending page from his exercise book and Alexander had to start again. Such an action I can understand might have been a salutary lesson for a normal child, but for one who couldn't follow the standard sequencing of a text without jumbling it, this task took on the proportions of cleaning out the Aegean Stables. It did not improve his knowledge of the subject one bit: in fact, it probably served the purpose of alienating him from it instead. As the evening wore on we were torn about what to do. Should we tell him not to bother finishing, write it out ourselves, and compose an explanatory letter to his teacher? Would this look as if we were undermining his authority? Respect for his teachers was something that we have always been keen to maintain, and we did not want to affect Alexander's attitude, as it is necessary to believe in the competence of those doing the teaching in order to get anywhere.

Another problem current throughout his time in the lower school was the attitude of his teachers to spelling. The children were given weekly lists of words to learn. Those they got wrong had to be written out up to ten times each at break. As a mother I found this particularly distressing and symbolic, for as he made many mistakes, Alexander would have to miss his school milk in order mindlessly to copy out words. I knew that no matter how many times he wrote them, the process would never teach him how to spell: it just does not work that way with dyslexics.

Andrew and I thought we ought to contact the headmaster again before things got out of hand. As there was a staff training session scheduled on dyslexia, we felt it would be better to wait until after this event. We wanted to allow the teachers time for reflection. Many of them had clearly received no formal instruction on the nature of this disability. It was therefore, perhaps, unfair to expect them to be aware of how to present material to such children in an accessible form and to allow them to achieve, without being judged on their writing, which is merely the medium of presentation itself.

Training day came and was by all accounts excellent. Mr Pascal, a specialist in the field, gave a first rate exposition of what dyslexia was and what it meant in real terms. He also suggested a number of things that could be done for dyslexics in the school. Much of what he said applied directly to Alexander's situation.

Inspired by Mr Pascal's belief that dyslexics could achieve in a school environment if the correct approach was adopted, Andrew wrote to the headmaster of the lower school in late

October, outlining Alexander's problems, his strengths and alternative approaches that would help him. We made it very clear that we were grateful for the efforts of the staff and that we understood that Alexander's inability to achieve on paper, the conventional means of expression in school, must be very hard for them. What we wanted was the acceptance of alternative ways of presentation of work – both to him and from him. Could he stick work sheets into his book instead of copying them out? Could he present his home work essays on tape with a transcript provided by us? As Andrew said in his letter – 'unless the structure within which he operates is revised to take his difficulties into account, he will achieve very little and become even more unhappy'.

After this we again met the headmaster, who was very sympathetic to our position. He appreciated that the school system of rewards gave Alexander, in spite of his valuable oral contribution in lessons, no opportunity for public esteem. Although his contemporaries signed the good work book on a regular basis, there was no likelihood that Alexander would do so under present arrangements. The names of pupils who signed the book were published in a regular weekly bulletin which also gave details of special achievements by individuals together with administrative arrangements, competition and sporting results. Recurring names of achievers were noticed by other parents to whom the bulletin was circulated via pupil post every Friday.

The headmaster assured us that he would talk to the staff concerned to see what modifications could be made and one result which we were very pleased to see was that in the bulletin in December Alexander had signed the good work book for his class talk.

Daily living with Alexander took up so much of our emotional energy – just to ensure that he was all right – that a year had gone by and we still had not followed up all the avenues suggested by Mr Freeland and Mrs Urry. Mr Freeland's report had indicated a phonological difficulty in manipulating the sound system of language. Mrs Urry had recommended assessment by a speech therapist for a closer look at his language. These combined professional awarenesses struck a chord with us, for when Alexander was about four years old, I had been concerned that his speech, while precise in its definition, was often slurred. I arranged for him to see a speech and drama teacher. She thought that he was too young for lessons and that the basic problem was that his brain was working faster than his tongue: we would have to keep reminding him to speak clearly. Nevertheless, prompted by others that it might be appropriate to seek help in this area, we went to see a local authority speech therapist during half term. The tests applied, though, seemed to us rather basic and consisted largely of him being asked to identify verbally objects on flash cards. The conclusions were that his vocabulary was wide and that there was basically nothing wrong with his speech. I supposed such assessments were really aimed at those who had difficulty in actually speaking at all. As we had so much else to tackle, we thought that this was one matter which we would allow to drop, for as Alexander could actually communicate perfectly well orally, any phonological inconsistencies were really fine tuning with which we didn't need to overload him.

December arrived and with it his first end of term report. In Maths he had come 22nd out of 22 both in his class and examination performance. In English he was 18th for his term work and 11th in the examination. His English teacher commented on his strength in oral aspects – with his mature vocabulary and good powers of expression, but said that it was difficult to make fair allowances for his genuine problems with written work. This was the same pattern across all subjects: there was praise for his knowledge, understanding and contribution to class discussion combined with an awareness that he could not achieve on paper.

It was all very well letting Alexander do GCSE course work, but preparations had to be made for him to enter the examination officially. As it unfortunately proved impossible to make the appropriate arrangements at his school, I inquired about the possibility of his entering as an external candidate at Fareham College.

I had an interview with the vice principal who was most sympathetic to Alexander's position. He understood clearly his desire to achieve in the face of disability and Fareham College was certainly the place capable of facilitating this, provided that the examination board would agree to accept him. A member of the English department – Mrs Elisabeth Wade – took responsibility for his file, in that she marked his work so far and would be setting his unseen and supervised texts and essays. As she had no experience of his working method, it seemed a good idea for her to see him in action.

I bought the BBC *Macbeth* cartoon book and tape in the same series as the *Othello* that had started the whole thing. This time, for once, I had to pay the full price. It was not a bargain, but it was certainly worth it! Alexander read and listened to it one evening. The next day Mrs Wade put questions – which he had not previously seen – to him.

I was nervous as I began to read the transcript of his answers because Alexander had never really had the opportunity to talk to other people about literature at this level before. Although I knew that he'd enjoyed the play, I was concerned in case he did not respond naturally in front of someone else in a formal situation. I needn't have worried; here is his answer to one of the questions she asked him on that day:

'Explain this passage from Act I scene 2:

> For brave Macbeth – well he deserves that name –
> Disdaining fortune, with his brandished steel,
> Which smoked with bloody execution
> Like valour's minion carved out his passage.

'The soldier is describing Macbeth's bravery and that he deserves the name "brave" and that "disdaining fortune" is fighting against the great forces of Norway and the rebels of Scotland. He is disdaining against what might happen at the end of the battle, fighting with all his strength. "And with his brandished steel" means the sword he was using and brandishing, waving it in massive triumph. "Which smoked with bloody execution": the scientific view of this part is blood is hot, the red part of blood is hot, but I think Shakespeare put it as the blood of the anger of the soldiers – their wrath, and the joy of battle. He talks about his sword as "like valour's minion carved out his passage", his sword is his chief weapon; it is also like a main servant and the valour – his bravery and his courage against the rebels and the Norwegians. And "carved out his passage" – his sword cutting through the Norweyan ranks like a knife through bread.'

The next step was to convince the examination board. Their first response was cautious, explaining that GCSE had been increasingly linked with testing at Key Stage 4 – in other words, sixteen plus – whereas Alexander was below Key Stage 2. The board needed his reports for consideration and clarification of the assessment procedures that would be followed in his case so that they and the college could not only be, but be seen to be, above criticism in such an unusual case. They made it clear as an opening position that course work offered entirely on tape, or entirely transcribed by a third person, would not be acceptable.

We provided the examinations officer at Fareham College, Mrs Harding, with all the information and documentary evidence about Alexander that we had at hand: reports from the educational psychologist, orthoptist and occupational therapist, together with a sample of his handwriting. We sent the poem *The Imprisonment of Persephone* in a typed version and in his handwriting (see Figure 1) to show the contrast between the quality of his mind and his inability to communicate on paper – not that he could actually have *thought* these ideas onto paper in the first place. As the dyslexic report, though still current for examination purposes was one and a half years old, Celia Darbyshire, the educational psychologist at Fareham College read all the reports and produced a summary of them for the examination board, together with her opinion of Alexander's position.

She said that the reports indicated that although Alexander was of a very superior intelligence, he was clumsy, with inaccurate control of his eyes, which in turn led to difficulties with hand–eye coordination. She explained that the resulting handwriting problems, together with his poor spelling, limited his ability to express himself in writing. Her recommendation was that ideally he should be allowed to complete his GCSE work orally and that it should then be transcribed verbatim.

Students at Fareham College are really very lucky. Alexander's detailed assessment cost us a fortune. I've heard that

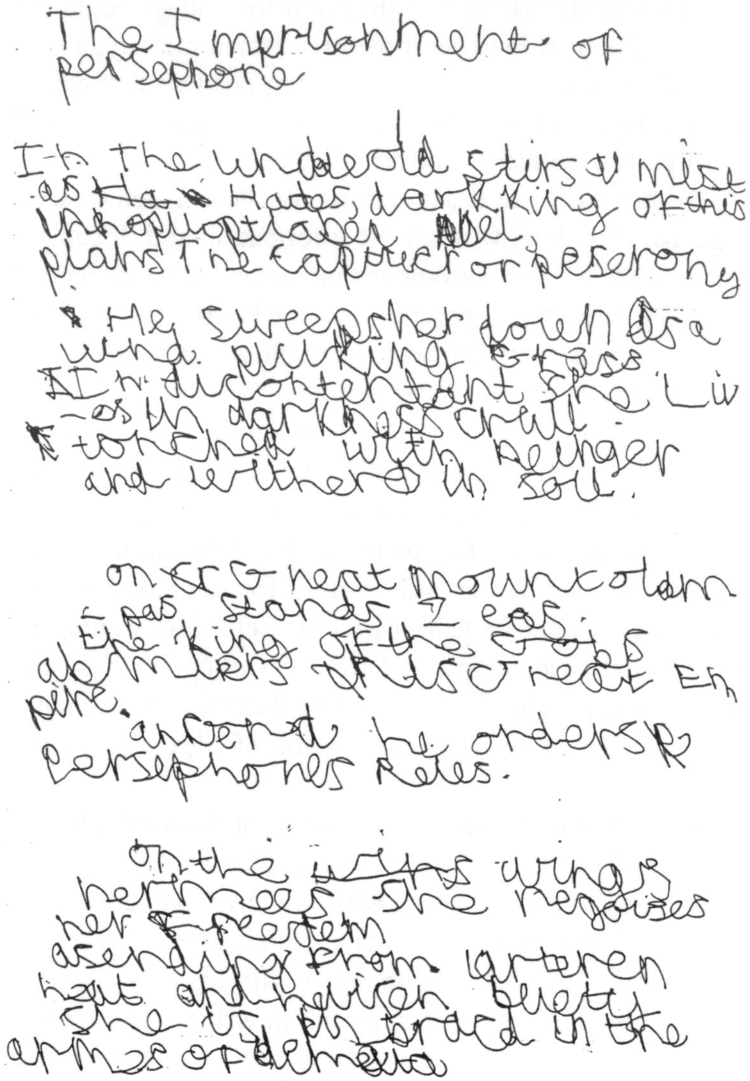

Figure 1 The Imprisonment of Persephone *in Alexander's* handwriting

pupils in the school state system have had to wait incredible periods of time for assessment: Fareham students have the services of an on-site educational psychologist who tests those thought dyslexic. She then produces a short report highlighting their strengths and weaknesses, making recommendations as to how these should be considered by examination boards.

Mrs Harding was now in a position to write back to the SEG (Southern Examining Group) in full. She assured them that although he was not as old as others who had entered for this examination, his age did not affect either his performance in, or his enjoyment of, the subject: indeed, to be awarded a GCSE would give Alexander a boost to the flagging self-esteem that accompanied his dyslexic weaknesses.

The college offered every assurance that I would have nothing to do with the assessment of any material. In order to verify the authenticity of the work, it was explained that: everything was recorded on tape *as* Alexander composed it; arrangements had been made for an independent member of the English department to set and administer the supervised unseen assignment which would take place in college. In effect, the checks and controls on Alexander's work were substantially more rigorous than on other students.

Mrs Harding asked for further advice on which method of presentation would be acceptable – original tapes *and* transcripts would be provided, but if the board insisted, Alexander could provide handwritten versions as well, although this labour would be inauthentic, as the analytical response to the literature had already taken place and been accurately recorded.

The week spent waiting for the reply seemed an eternity, for I knew that the decision of the board on this issue would directly affect Alexander's whole future. The letter came: we had the green light. The SEG had accepted the college's assurances that I would not be involved in Alexander's assessment. The only drawback was that at least a third was required to be written out in Alexander's hand – the rest he could type or word process. As he could do neither of these things, it meant that Alexander had to write out the whole of his course work – a horrendous task, the results of which no one could read. We were also told that we could produce another copy of any work which was not clearly written or readily readable, for clarification purposes. In effect, Alexander's file would now consist of tapes, transcripts and handwritten versions. It was also requested that the work should be included in the sample presented for moderation.

Although getting Alexander to write out pages of illegible material would be another Herculean labour, I was extremely grateful to the SEG for accepting such an unusual case and enabling Alexander to fulfil his potential as the educational psychologist, Mr Freeland, had so correctly advised.

Composing the essays had been great fun from Alexander's perspective, but I knew that in order to persuade him of the necessity of writing them out, I would have to tell him what he was actually doing. I was worried about altering the chemistry of something that was working so well, but he was absolutely thrilled at the discovery that he had already completed most of a GCSE without even realising it.

The next hurdle was the syllabus requirement for Alexander to complete an unseen, supervised response. I drove him to Fareham College one afternoon and left him for a couple of hours with Mrs Wade while I paced the corridors and frequented the coffee bars like an expectant father. At last he emerged: both he and Mrs Wade were smiling. I was to take him home for tea and then bring him back in the early evening so that she could play him back the tape, word by word, and he could write it out.

Mrs Wade had first read to him, and then asked questions about, *Dulce et Decorum Est* by Wilfred Owen and *The Soldier* by Rupert Brooke. When I eventually got to see a transcript of the whole proceedings I was, even though I knew him so well, impressed by the maturity and originality of his response to unseen material under unaccustomed conditions. One of the questions Mrs Wade has asked was 'What do you find of special interest in the language of the poem? Are there any unusual or particularly effective uses of words or images?' His answer to this was long and detailed, but my favourite part was where he was able to accurately identify the urgency of action in relation to the word 'clumsy' in the Owen poem: '"fitting the clumsy helmets just in time" – it refers to *them* doing it clumsily, [rather] than to the helmets, since this is probably because they had not strapped them on hard enough in time for the bombs to come down. It does not actually refer to the helmets being clumsy.'

The file was nearly complete. Alexander decided to include a piece of original writing, *The Imprisonment of Persephone* (see the Appendix), as the syllabus allowed for a creative response inspired by the study of works of literature. This poem had been prompted by the Greek myths he had read at school.

For another piece Alexander was asked if he could see any common theme in some of the books he liked and he chose attitudes to death in *Jane Eyre*, *Macbeth* and *The Hobbit*. I thought his selection to be a fairly eclectic combination, but he ingeniously explored it from the angle of depth and emptiness. In Helen Burns' death in *Jane Eyre* he saw a fullness: 'Helen wants to die because she will be happy afterwards, since death is the eternal life, enriched with the joy of mortality, but eternally'.

He compared this with the empty deaths of the characters in *Macbeth* who were unprepared to meet their end. He commented that even though Macbeth himself knew that he was going to die, 'his warlike challenge at the end is in fact to protect himself from his fear of death both physically and mentally: 'I will not yield,/ To kiss the ground before young Malcolm's feet/ And to be baited with the rabble's curse.' His warlike valour in shouting these challenging words gives him the courage inside to attack Macduff outwardly.'

He went on to observe that whereas *Jane Eyre* and *Macbeth* were set in a world that was recognisably our own, *The Hobbit* was set in a fantasy world: 'Normally a death in an unreal world wouldn't upset me, but Tolkien has the power to move me; the main death is that of Thorin, clouded with remorse and unhappiness.'

Here was Alexander, three years on from when he had first wept at Thorin's death; now, untaught, he was able to analyse the power behind the words that had so moved him:

> 'It is powerful since Thorin had been guiding the company and the reader through their adventures. He has been strong, noble and kind. We have seen his courage repeatedly, as in the battle of the five armies when he led the forces of men, dwarves, and elves. "Thorin wielded his axe with mighty strokes and nothing seemed to harm him. 'To me! To me! Elves and Men! To me! O my kinsfolk!' he cried, and his voice shook like a horn in the valley."

The language is rousing and stirring; it excites me, and makes me respect his power and his courage. His death is therefore tragic, since Tolkien has made me feel part of the company that Thorin has been leading.

The death scene of Thorin contains a mixture of emotions. First, there is Gandalf's obvious pleasure of finding Bilbo alive. Then there is the shock to Bilbo and ourselves of finding Thorin laid out on the bed heavily wounded:

> "There indeed lay Thorin Oakenshield, wounded with many wounds, and his rent armour and notched axe were cast upon the floor."

Here the repetition of "wounds" shows the seriousness of his injuries, and the armour, which had previously "gleamed with the sun and splendour" of the dwarvish craftmakers was twisted and broken, and discarded upon the floor.

The contrast between the former splendour and the present bent and broken object made me feel sorrowful. In his final words, he apologises for his words and deeds at the gate and praises Bilbo for his courage.

Although in respect of the need to clear his conscience, this death scene is similar to Mrs Reed's, it is different, in that my sympathy goes to Thorin, and not to Mrs Reed, because there is genuine affection between Bilbo and Thorin.'

Alexander completed his course work file in March 1992, a month after his ninth birthday. For his final essay he tried a different, protagonistic approach whereby he adopted the persona of three characters in *Jane Eyre* and described Jane through their eyes. It was a relief to have finished the content of the file, but Alexander's labour in transcribing pages in his own hand still took another couple of weeks. We now faced a wait of five months until August for the results.

In many aspects of his life Alexander shared characteristic traits with other boys. He pestered us for a Master System – we refused because we saw it as a reductive approach to entertainment. He saved up his birthday, Christmas and pocket money and bought one himself. He would, however, lose interest after half an hour's play, and it was Andrew who became the main devotee of 'Alex Kidd'!

In the lower school Alexander remade the acquaintance of a boy he had been friendly with at nursery but had not seen for four years. This boy was a year older than him but they became – and still are today – firm friends. They had so much in common – intelligence, interest in topics other than football and cartoons and at school were the butt of horrible bullying.

The ducks, Rose and Mabel had started laying eggs – one each on alternate days. On principle I never buy eggs, for if battery, they are produced under disgusting conditions and, I once cracked open a free range one that was fertilized and developing – never again! The children savoured the delights of fresh, really fresh, omelettes and soufflés. Rose and Mabel were happy and tame. Their wings had grown, but as they made no attempt to fly away there was no need to use the moveable pen any more. They roamed free in the garden rummaging for wood lice and slugs and came when they were called. I liked them for their independence and felt honoured that such diffident creatures would come for a cuddle!

I felt the ducks added a deeper reality to the children's lives and wanted them each to have another pet. At first I wanted sheep, but a cautionary tale from a colleague about maggots soon put me off that idea. Then I hit on it – pygmy goats. I researched the topic with care and found that wethers made the best pets: billy goats were clearly impossible, and nanny goats made a terrible din calling for a mate whenever they came into season.

We joined the Pygmy Goat Club and read all the literature. We contacted numerous breeders in order to book ourselves two wethers. At Easter I had a telephone call from a lady nearby who had three males and two females. We were asked to come to pick the ones we wanted and return three months later when they were weaned.

The shed at the bottom of the garden needed some working on. We built them a little den to sleep in, erected 'benches' made from wine boxes and my father built a hay rack. The concrete area adjoining had to be fenced off to provide an all-weather play area. We dragged in some toys – heavy branches for the goats to play on and peel the bark from, and wooden platforms to jump on. We bought straw, hay, concentrated food, bowls, brushes and scissors to cut their hooves, which grow like toe nails.

Emily thought that Edward would be a good name for her goat and Alexander chose Bonkers for his. We all went to collect the boys, as we referred to them – in late June. Although I'd earmarked two of the three, the other one had not been sold, so the children had a choice. Alexander picked a slim black and white one which looked rather more like a dog, and Emily chose a more solid and goat-like creature whose name – Edward – suited him well.

Their characters were clearly differentiated: Bonkers had a keen intelligence whereas Edward was definitely a plodder. It was raining one day when I took them a juicy weed each.

Bonkers took his into the shed to eat, whereas Edward stood munching in the rain crying – 'Maair' – because he was getting wet!

Rose and Mabel established dominance at once by attacking the newcomers. It would have been interesting to see how this relationship developed, but within a week tragedy struck. I had just let the ducks out for their morning slug hunt when I heard a frantic Emily yelling in terror. Mabel, neck at full stretch, was emitting terrified honking noises and Rose was nowhere to be seen. Between sobs Emily told me that a fox had run off with her. I gathered up the traumatised Mabel and I found Rose, who seemed to me to be in two pieces, abandoned, alive, but bleeding heavily. I rushed her to the vet to be put down. To my amazement he sewed her back together again and sent me away with antibiotics to pour down her beak twice daily.

Keeping the ducks was now impossible. It seemed cruel to imprison them but they could only be allowed out if we stood guard. Now the fox knew of their existence he would be back. Reluctantly, I donated them to a local farm trail. The children insisted on visiting them regularly, at extortionate expense, until one Saturday they just weren't there any more. No one knew where they had gone, but apparently a fox had been on the prowl.

Eurodisney opened early in 1992 and I wanted to take Alexander. We didn't have enough money for a family holiday, so I researched the possibilities and found a firm – Davies World Travel – which ran day trips. The cost, just over a hundred pounds all inclusive for the two of us, was very reasonable. We left at nine on Friday night and arrived at Eurodisney after twelve long hours on the coach on July 4th. We stayed in the sweltering heat until nearly midnight, and got home early on Sunday morning with very sore feet.

I can't say that it was my chosen way of spending a weekend, but Alexander loved it, particularly one hair-raising ride called the Pirates of the Caribbean. Given all of his differences from other children, I felt that it was important to give him experiences truly related to modern childhood that would form part of his consciousness and that he could talk about to others in the playground.

His end of year report was interesting: he had maintained his 11/22 position in English for the exam, but had sunk to 20th for his term performance, while his teacher commented on how he had continued to impress with his oral ability, general knowledge, and wide vocabulary. His effort and contribution to class discussion were given credit across the subjects, but in externally verifiable results – his actual attainment marks – he was doing considerably worse. It is on attainment, not effort, in our society that one is ultimately judged.

As the previous summer's entertainment had centred around the antics of Rose and Mabel, so this year's revolved around the goats. It was amazing what they would eat – grass, twigs, leaves, weeds, paper – even our clothes! Having an ice lolly in the garden became a very ecologically sound project as the boys would first munch the paper wrappers and then wait for us to finish so they could chew on the sticks. One day, Bonkers was sitting on my lap, nuzzling into my neck in a very affectionate manner – he was my friend! Then to my horror I felt hot goat's breath in my ear and realised that he was eating my hair!

It was an idyllic summer, but my anxiety mounted as August 27th – results day – drew nearer. From my reading of his work I knew that it was clearly GCSE standard, but I was worried in case some other objections to his age or method of working should be raised that would prevent him from being awarded his qualification.

To save him anxiety, I had kept my concerns from Alexander, and had not even told him when the results would be published. Instead, I went alone to the college first thing in the morning and waited while the grades were posted on the board; my finger shook as I followed the line along from his name, and then double checked it. He had passed with a grade B.

I phoned Andrew and heard a whoop of joy in the background from Alexander who had heard on the radio that it was GCSE results day. I was so excited on my way home that I got into the wrong lane on the motorway and had to make a long detour.

During the morning it became clear that Alexander's story was very newsworthy. In considering what press exposure should be welcomed, our main concern was that the determining factor in Alexander's future should be his intelligence and not his disability: publicity for his achievement could only be to his advantage.

The afternoon was therefore spent in television, radio and newspaper interviews. In Portsmouth, the news vendors' placards read 'City Wonder Kid Makes Grade' and his story took up most of the front page of the local paper. For the television reporters we had to keep walking through the college doors to locate his grade on the board, until the camera crew was satisfied with the best reaction shot. For us, however, the most telling thing happened on radio. Alexander was asked if he had any plans for the future.

'Yes,' he replied. 'I'm going to start my 'A' level now.'

It was the first we'd heard of it!

Alexander's Account:

This chapter chronicles a very important stage in my academic and mental development. I hope that the events I have selected will serve to give an accurate impression of my experiences, both painful and pleasurable, and the dramatic changes that occurred at an even more dramatic speed.

When I was still in the pre-prep, I obtained my parents' *Othello* cassettes and fully illustrated full text, and set about reading and listening to it simultaneously (a method which was later to serve me in good stead). The things that first attracted me to the story are things that most other boys are attracted by – the valour, the fighting and the soldiers. I began to analyse the plot, the language and the reasons for the meanings, and how the meanings were expressed, which my parents were quite impressed with.

This was the second great milestone to my academic achievement and shows how my my mind developed quickly away from the school. My parents asked me to talk about the play on tape. They then showed me more new texts and plays over a long space of time between the summer of 1991 and the spring of 1992. I didn't understand why this was, but the poems and plays I read expanded my mind, and made me see that there was a world beyond the petty expanse that I had to endure daily of games monitors and the like. They made all that I had to cope with in the ordinary seem irrelevant, because they gave me insights into things, such as evil, as being not just extant phenomena: there are causes, effects and solutions. Life cannot just be tackled by attacking a surface but by digging out the root. Thus I learnt that it was no use, for instance, to fight the immediate actions of the bully but to see why he did it.

One of the poems which brought me to this conclusion was John Donne's *A Hymn to God the Father*. Donne traces sin and evil to a source, namely original sin, and shows how it flourishes through himself, and from himself through others. I'm not suggesting that their bullying was occasioned by original sin, but that it had its roots in their personality.

At the beginning of the spring term in 1992 my parents finally let out the secret to me: I had been doing a GCSE. The sense of achievement that I felt at that moment had been matched by nothing that had ever gone in my life before, not even the acceptance into MENSA! However, this was slightly dulled by the fact that the examination board, as kind as they had been, required me to write in my own hand the essays which I had been producing for the course work.

One of my most vivid memories of this is sitting at my desk in my room as I am doing now, and writing out frantically the words from my recorded essays and my father's typescripts at the same time as my father was typing downstairs, which I could hear quite clearly.

However, there was not much time to rejoice in, since I had an examination to do in a few days. I had to go to Fareham College where I wrote my unseen examination. A point that I felt may not have been quite so good then, I consider to be a very important one now. In *Dulce et Decorum Est* there is a line in which 'clumsy helmets' are referred to. My point was it is not the helmets that are clumsy, but the men themselves, and that they must find a focus for their aggression and disappointment, as well as fear. However, after I had done the essay, the affair was not over. Even though I went away after, I had to come back again in the evening to write the whole thing up.

On the way there in the car, my mother said that she had a surprise gift for me when I reached home after doing the writing. I remembered a rather brief reference that I'd heard in a cassette called *Journey into Space*, the old parlour game about animal, vegetable and mineral, and thus proceeded to ask her questions such as is it an animal, is it a vegetable, is it mechanical?

After several hours of writing and listening to the tape (sometimes simultaneously) my mother drove me home. After having my bath, I received my present, a bow, two arrows with sucker ends, and a plastic knife. I remember putting my pyjama trousers on and leaping around the corridor firing the arrows off at the ceiling! It seemed an ideal ending to a difficult day.

So far in this chapter, I have concentrated on the GCSE. But the GCSE was only one part, though a major one, of my life at that time. Perhaps the greater thing that dominated it, though I feel not the most important, even though it had greater impact, was my entrance into the lower school in the autumn of 1991.

On my first day at the school, I had great hopes. I remember saying to my father on the way that this would give me new opportunities, new advantages. I would be able to express myself fully at last. I assumed, because this was a higher part of the school, I would have greater opportunity to show my talents.

When I reached the school, there was a great sense of confusion in the air, as all age groups were crammed up staircases in the hope of getting them organised without any attendants on them. Crushed like a grape at harvest time in the south of France, I thought this, in my naïveté, to be part of a great tradition, and to be the start of better things to come. I temporarily (I then thought, permanently) decided to adopt the regime of the school not just outwardly, but inwardly.

This worked okay for the first term, with my occasional successes in getting into the 'good work book', the standard by which academic success was measured; but my increasing failure at sport emerged among my contemporaries, who for a time had forgotten it in their elation in being accepted into a regime which fitted them like a glove, or, as they would probably have it, a football boot (I know my wit is deficient). As the terms progressed, not only my sporting lack of prowess, but my academic (as far as the school was concerned) failures also appeared. To begin with, the teachers made attempts to help me in a good natured sort of way, perhaps in the hope that my dyslexia would go away. I am sure they thought of it as a temporary thing which could be sorted out, not realising that you couldn't cure it. My form teacher, who also took me for English and Maths devised a system in which I had various coloured squares with numbers on them and had to place them where numbers should go when trying to do long division, multiplication, and subtraction. This sounded like a good idea, since it stopped the handwriting difficulty, but it took me more time to find the squares than it would have taken me to print, as neatly as I could, all the figures that were needed. So the scheme had to be abandoned. The result was that he gave me a 'D' in Maths at the end of term, and told me to try harder, for I was using my dyslexia as an excuse for laziness and that it wasn't the problem my parents and I were making it out to be.

For my other academic shortcomings, as they saw them, they devised other systems, including the traditional methods, such as writing out, five or ten times each, spellings which I got wrong. Also, because I was so slow at my work, I had to come in during my break times and copy out from the board things which I had been not able fully to write down before. This mainly occurred as a result of the History lessons last thing on a Thursday: on Fridays I had to miss morning break, and sometimes part of lunch, to copy out laboriously every word which the teacher had written on the board: these were not just rough notes, but almost short essays.

The other thing which got even worse was my handwriting, as I was expected to write at speed. At this point, a normally well meaning and kind science teacher ripped out several pages of my work in front of the entire class because he thought them not to be sufficiently neat, and I had copied them in the wrong order. I felt humiliated in front of the others, not only by their standards, but also more dejected in my own mind, because I felt in myself that I had failed in some way and was deficient.

Against this background, the GCSE made an amazing contribution to my life. It was a way of making me feel separate from my contemporaries, but in a positive sense, something I had never felt before. It made me give up trying to break their code, and to construct my own instead.

I would like to talk about the bullying which was so terrible during these years. Because of my continued non-conformity to their standards, I became, again, recipient not only of the paltry but effective verbal abuse to which I had been accustomed, but also of a new intensified, physical threat, even worse than before. Early attempts to solve the problem by staff, though firm, were on the whole ineffective, and after I had complained, the bullying intensified in reprisals and acts of revenge by my fellow 'lowers'. As I kept coming back with more and more complaints of such, including being punched and kicked in sensitive areas, less and less was done. I feel I was marked off in the mental register of some of my teachers as over sensitive and a nuisance. I think partly that they did not believe all that I was saying, not because it was improbable, but because I was claiming (truly) that so much was happening. I can, to a certain extent, see their predicament, but I cannot excuse in my own mind their lack of action.

I remember being advised to ignore the problem, to just be silent, as the bullies would soon lose interest. When someone hits you, you can't just forget about it, and if he slams you against a wall there is nothing you can do to ignore it. I discovered that the only strategy that was worth employing was to push my 'comrade' away and run like Linford Christie (though not, as you may have gathered, at quite that speed).

I did have other distractions, besides the GCSE, to keep my mind off this 'part of growing up'. My parents bought my sister and me two ducks which Emily forcefully tamed by running around after them in a pen for about half an hour one day during the summer. I enjoyed dealing with living beings which weren't vicious, and which, even though they were difficult to understand, could be comprehended. I felt that they liked me, which is more than I can say of my class mates.

Besides my rural pleasures, I was also able to make a new friend, or rather, re-enter a friendship which had started at nursery school, but had been cut of when my friend and I went to different schools. He was also very seriously bullied, and this gave me a common link with him, a very strong one, since he had also endured both verbal and physical bullying, as well as a general isolation from most of his contemporaries. He provided me with stability, when all else around me was uncertain: for one minute, I might gain brief acceptance by the group, and the next be repulsed to the periphery. He was someone who wanted to learn more, without having to sift through the 'facts' that the school bombarded us with – he had an imagination, and like me, wanted to function independently from the 'standard product' of the school's regime.

I received my GCSE results during the summer. It was a very special day as it was the first time I had ever appeared on television. We were interviewed at Fareham College by both South Today and TVS, but only appeared on the latter's evening programme. There was a reception at Fareham College which my friend was unfortunately unable to attend, but at which the drinks were flowing (except in my direction) and there was understandably a general air of celebration. However, this was not the end, for on the day of the results, I started petitioning my parents, of course in the most genteel manner, to allow me to do an 'A' level. I felt not only that it would be the logical step but that GCSE had raised my standard of thinking and helped me put the concerns of my contemporaries in perspective. They would feel great sorrow if they kicked a football the wrong way, but I had learned about the real sorrows of death, love, hate, kindness, greed, treachery, avarice, power and corruption. I could learn more about life from reading poetry than I could by trying to kick a large spherical object between two metal posts. I no longer had to measure myself against their immediate, and very confined, boundaries. I had started to find out about the complex working of the human mind, and didn't want it to stop there.

CHAPTER FIVE

'A' level

My father, not normally one to court public attention, thoroughly enjoyed Alexander's success, and surprised us all by doing a tour of the local newsagents the day after the GCSE results asking for the placards – we framed the two in the best condition and they hang in Alexander's bedroom at home and in my parents' house.

We held an impromptu party to celebrate. One of the guests was a favourite tutor from our Sussex University days (where Andrew and I met) – Stephen Medcalf. We sought his advice on Alexander's future and he told us without hesitation to get him into a special school. We were initially horrified because the whole point in doing GCSE had been to concentrate on his strengths and not his weaknesses: this, however, was not what Stephen had meant – he had implied a good quality public school. He suggested Winchester College.

We had not previously considered a boarding school for Alexander – I suppose our thinking was that there seemed little point in having a child if we were going to give him away for other people to bring up. It had been our hope that we could maintain continuity in our children's education by keeping them at the same school from the age of four right up to eighteen. However, Alexander was clearly not happy at this stage in his schooling, nor was he achieving in the school's terms. Over the next few days we considered Stephen's suggestion – for, after all, transfer wouldn't be immediate. It seemed a good idea to be informed of what was available for someone of his calibre, and Winchester was only about half an hour away.

The three of us went for an interview at Winchester on a beautiful Saturday that autumn with Mr Peter Roberts, the master in charge of scholars. Alexander loved the place and was particularly tickled by the ancient graffiti – Thomas Browne (later to be Sir Thomas Browne of *Religio Medici*) had carved his name in the scholars' room – the very room he hoped to inhabit!

Mr Roberts thought that we should consider entry for Alexander a year early – at 12 instead of 13+. He explained the mechanics of the scholarship examination – but this was designed for very intelligent normal boys, and Alexander certainly wasn't conventional! We inquired whether he might be admitted on the basis of his 'A' level result instead. Amused by the novel character of our approach, Mr Roberts said that this was something which could be discussed nearer the time. He added that as the period for scholarship assessment took several days, those testing him would have plenty of time to come to terms with his oral ability.

Alexander's excitement was tangible, for here seemed a sympathetic alternative educational environment to the one in which he had been so unhappy during the previous year. It was a ray of hope which gave another dimension to his perception of his existence at school.

Starting the 'A' level that Alexander wanted was a massive undertaking on all fronts. Apart from the stimulation of his home environment, in which discussions about literature are as common as those about colour schemes would be in the homes of interior designers, Alexander was completely un-taught. The GCSE had been his own natural response to the texts without the critical analytical skills which are usually taught in basic form at this stage. This meant that, in technical respects, the acknowledged gap between GCSE and 'A' level would be even greater in his case. There remained the questions of which syllabus to follow and how to get the examination board to accept his method of working – not just for the course work, but for the papers to be sat in the examination room.

We had to begin somewhere, and the best way seemed to be to start teaching him on the assumption that something could be worked out, rather than delaying his eager mind while negotiations were conducted. It was simultaneously an exciting prospect and a minefield containing potential haz-ards. I was determined to go against the current trend of student-centred learning. I opted instead for solid teaching, on the principle that you cannot construct a building without bricks. I am convinced that if you give students a solid grounding, they will have the mental structure and discipline to explore topics by themselves from an informed stand-point, rather than one which only allows them to explore their 'feelings' towards a text.

We launched the course, with figures of speech – similes, metaphors, personification and so on – not just seeing how to *spot* them in a text, but always *how* they worked – what *effect* they were achieving. This very early basic training has imprinted itself on Alexander's approach to academic work, in that it is second nature to him to look for causal reasons in all aspects of study, rather than just noticing their presence and effect on him.

We then progressed to Tillyard's *The Elizabethan World Picture* and its concentration of parallel hierarchies throughout creation through the humours, elements, chain of being and human society. Alexander found this way of looking at the world fascinating and relevant, in that so much of that early thought actually made sense today – it even helped him a couple of years later with his biology homework where he had to explain the structure of the organic kingdoms.

From here we moved on to Elizabethan poetry and sonnets, studying the interconnections between form and content, where various aspects of a topic are progressively explored within a framework. He seemed to understand and enjoy what we had covered, but to make sure that the material was really assimilated, I asked him to write one – to pick a particular sonnet framework – Italian, English, Shakespearian or Spenserian – and work within it. The result was *The Eagle*, which encapsulated his understanding of Tillyard, his application of it to a natural order that is extant today, and an ability to work within the paradoxically liberating confines of sonnet form. He was still only nine years old. This poem, together with another sonnet and his commentary, formed one of his pieces of 'A' level course work.

In his commentary, Alexander wrote:

> 'I have always been fascinated by hierarchies and my understanding of the natural order was deepened by studying ideas from Tillyard's *Elizabethan World Picture*. As well as exploring this in my essays, I decided to express it in sonnet form. At the top of the ornithological rung of the ladder we see the eagle who

The Eagle

High in the air it soars in majesty
The eagle riding on the wind it reigns;
Nor air nor sun can fade its great beauty
As king of air it hovers over plains.
The patchwork of the plains delights his eyes,
The woods and forest beckon to reward
His piercing sight, which tears through their disguise,
As then with all his might he dives toward
The unsuspecting victim of the ground;
It writhes in pain within the eagle's claws
Unwilling, but by unsigned contract bound
To accept death within the eagle's jaws.
A shot rings out, the bird descends the sky
Like eagle and its prey we all must die.

[October 1992]

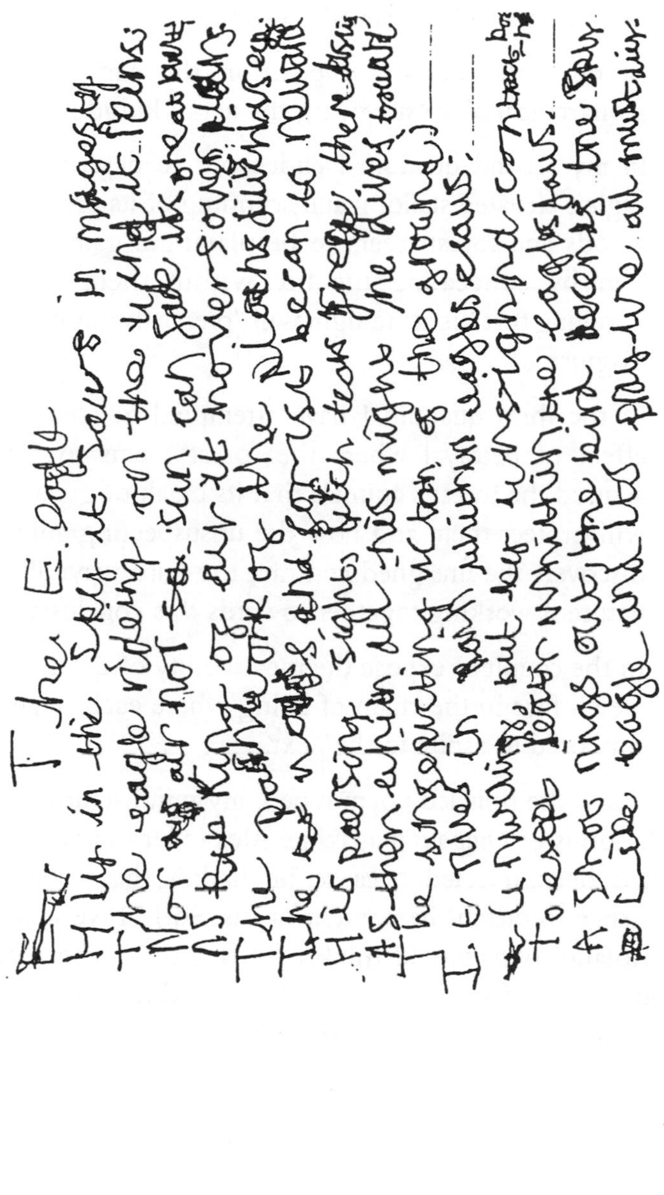

The E. Eagle

Figure 2 The Eagle *in Alexander's handwriting*

mercilessly kills its prey, its justification being an "unsigned contract" of instinctive natural position and desire. This is the basis of my sonnet.

In my first quatrain, I position the eagle in its monarchical place surveying the aerial kingdom.

In my second quatrain I endeavour to describe the eagle's elevated stalking and scanning of its prey. The woods and forests seem to be playing a game with him by concealing the life within them whilst knowing that his acute sight will "pierce through their disguise".

In the third quatrain I have attempted to create an effect of betrayal where the forest seems to have assured the forest's animals that its cloak of greenery will protect them and how the unsuspecting animal discovers the unsigned contract the hard way: all of nature is working together towards this conclusion.

In the couplet I expose the inevitability of death that we all face in the chain of being where each stage is supposed to aspire to the next.'

When I saw the finished poem typed, my mind returned to Roland Johns of *Outposts* magazine. Alexander's earlier poems had been rejected because he hadn't the technical competence to match the content of his work. I wondered what Roland Johns would think of it this time. The reply was quite a put down: we were told that whilst technique was a major element to poetry, there has to be an emotional content that derives from experience that one cannot have attained by the age of nine.

No mention of Alexander's achievement in GCSE was made in the weekly bulletin issued by the school. He was hurt and it took him a long time to accept that his ability and real achievement could not be accommodated in his school in the same way as the consequences of his disability were noted. I explained that in a way it was a good thing that his success hadn't been given public acclaim along with the school's blue and red badges and cycling proficiency awards, for it justified the effort that he was going to have to make over the next couple of years: if he couldn't be accepted on their terms, he would have to make his own. His 'A' level would have a tangible impact on his life and its merits would be recognised beyond the internally heralded rewards of his parochial school environment.

Fareham College seemed the most suitable location for Alexander formally to base his 'A' level and permission was sought and was forthcoming. As he was under sixteen, a letter from his current headmaster was required stating that he was aware of Alexander's studies at the College. The headmaster, before providing written confirmation, interviewed Andrew about any possible impact on Alexander's school work. He accepted the assurance that there would be none, as we planned that the teaching would take place at weekends. He asked if there was anything the school could do to help, and Andrew at once replied that there was: Alexander could be excused from the then obligatory Saturday morning sports. Relief all round followed this agreement, for not only would we have time to work in, but Alexander would be reprieved from the humiliation of these games, frequented by eagerly cheering parents coaching from the sidelines. My feelings on such occasions had been akin to the embarrassment of the sports day sack race, but rather worse as he was obviously letting his team down: whenever he missed the ball there were either sighs or silence from the onlookers as they tried to be understanding.

The 'A' level I chose for him was the AEB 660 syllabus which was at the time 50 per cent course work and 50 per cent examination. The course work element consisted of eight assignments and an extended essay. The usual practice with this syllabus was to include one or two essays from the first year's work, with the remainder from the second year, by which time the student would be producing more mature responses.

After much thought, I elected to approach things differently with Alexander and complete all the course work in the first year, when he would still be nine to ten years old. This would leave us free to concentrate on the examination texts (four books and study for an unseen critical appreciation paper) during the second year. My reasoning was that I had to balance his unique requirements against the advantages we could gain by submitting second year work. Course work can be revised by the student as many times as he wants before it is submitted, but an essay composed against the clock in an examination room has to be right first time round. I would have to teach Alexander the technique of producing a timed essay 'blind' onto tape in perfect form. Unlike the other students, he wouldn't be able either to see what he had written, or to go back to alter things. This was going to be a particular acquired skill that could not be allowed to become confused with the processes of writing course work essays.

The first year then, devoted entirely to course work, would be a time for education. He would learn from his study of the books and his mind would develop in ways that would enable him to tackle the examination texts the following year: it would be a foundation. That was the theory, and I believe that it worked.

Instead of being an external candidate, Alexander was enrolled as a proper student at Fareham. He wasn't full time, of course, but what is known as a flexi student. The very name sums up the college's flexible approach to education. We paid the college (or rather, my father did, as the cumulative cost of funding Alexander was already mounting beyond our ability to cover it) for nine hour blocks of lessons. We were charged half price as he was under eighteen, and the college then paid a lecturer to give him tuition for an hour a week.

Mrs Wade, who had helped with his GCSE, seemed the ideal choice. She knew Alexander and was firm and precise in her handling of him, qualities which were greatly appreciated as children need to know where they stand. It became her responsibility, through Fareham College's examinations' office and in consultation with us, to conduct negotiations with the examination board about Alexander's requirements. Before this could begin, we had to book another appointment with Mr Freeland, because the educational psychologist's report was now out of date for examination purposes.

While we waited for the appointment, we followed up yet another of the recommendations from the previous report – Alexander should be taught to touch type in preparation for being able to word process, an option which has worked for many children with dyslexia. At that time we thought this might be the way forward for him as an alternative to the tape recorder. My father, who always delights in finding articles in the newspaper that might be of interest to different members of the family, cut out for us an advertisement for the Amstrad NC 100 notepad computer which had just come on to the market. The computer was the size of an A4 sheet of paper: it weighed next to nothing and would be ideal for taking to school to use there. The advertisement had said that Amstrad would give a full refund if the purchaser couldn't be conversant with its basic functions within five minutes. My father said that if we thought it to be appropriate, he would buy it for Alexander's 'A' level along with a printer. Andrew researched this area as I know nothing about computers. As it seemed the easiest machine to use, the purchase was made.

The next task was to teach Alexander to touch type. We contacted all sorts of organisations, but none of the courses seemed appropriate to him. Then we struck gold – the Dyslexia Institute in Winchester actually ran courses specifically to teach children to touch type. The lessons ran for twenty weeks throughout the autumn and spring terms on Monday evenings. We were sceptical that anyone could make any impact teaching someone as uncoordinated as Alexander to touch type, but to our amazement, the lady who taught him, surely a saint for her patience against such odds, was able to encourage him to a surprising peak of seventeen words a minute on our old portable. Her policy was that children should learn on such machines before transferring their skills to a word processor.

Apart from the exhaustion involved in going to Winchester after school every week, and the additional practice required at home, the course ironically had two unforeseen beneficial consequences. First, although Alexander could just about touch type, it became apparent that he still could not *think* on to paper – the quality of his response was severely damaged by what was for him the unnatural effort of having consciously to control his fingers. His mind, quite simply, could not perform both functions at the same time – well, at least now we knew and we had to abandon our plans for him to take the Amstrad to school. Second, we now had a word processor and a printer, tools which were essential to process the course work essays efficiently. Without the flexibility of the word processor, Andrew would have had to type several versions until Alexander had perfected each essay. Before Alexander acquired the skill of composing succinctly on tape, his first versions of essays needed a great deal of attention and typing would have been a nightmare.

Information technology was not the solution to Alexander's problems, but I would certainly recommend such specialised lessons for other dyslexic children. Because each child is different, the burden of constant trial and error experimentation falls on parents, who are best placed to understand what is required, and need to persevere to find the optimum method for their own child.

We approached the second interview with the educational psychologist in an altogether different frame of mind from our first meeting with him. There was no uncertainty over the outcome and we already knew the extent of the problems all too well. This test was commissioned for the express purpose of definition for the examination board of the precise nature of his dyslexia, which made it impossible for him to present his material in the standard way. Mr Freeland was very curious to look at the developments that had taken place in Alexander. I quote here from the initial 'assessment' section of his report:

> 'I was very interested to meet Alex on a second occasion and with the knowledge that Alex had undertaken GCSE English Literature successfully. I was half anticipating a pupil whose development would be somewhat "lopsided". It was very reassuring to meet in Alex a calm, modest, well balanced pupil who has managed to integrate his unusual achievements very successfully into a modest self-presentation. I made reference with Alex to a

speech in *Othello,* the text of which I could barely remember. While the speech was not a key speech, Alex was able to pick up where my memory failed and took me through the entire speech, not by rote but by elaborating the concepts and the theme of the speech. Alex's natural facility with really quite high order concepts was very impressive indeed. It was very clear that Alex's understanding was at an extremely high level.

Alex showed an excellent orientation to assessment, being very clear on the reasons for coming to see me. Asking Alex about any difficulties he experiences, he commented that he has difficulty in keeping up with the pace of reading; has difficulties with Mathematics ("not my best subject"); has difficulty with spelling and written expression. With respect to the latter, Alex commented that he becomes very irritated when he cannot finish a specific piece of work and has to stay in at break time to do so. I asked Alex if he understood the nature of his learning difficulties and felt that he was not really sure where being dyslexic fits in to his overall image of himself and he certainly does not seem to use it as a self-attribution.'

The gap on the WISC test between his verbal and non-verbal IQ scales had increased to a staggering 37 points. The verbal scale now read 149, or 155 excluding the arithmetic sub test, equivalent, according to MENSA, to an IQ of 178 on their scale. If it had gone up that much after his untaught GCSE, we sometimes speculate what it might be now after two years of 'A' level and six months of a degree course, but finding out would be a luxury, not a necessity at this stage. In Mr Freeland's opinion the unevenness in the WISC verbal and performance scores did not present great cause for concern, as his ability for verbal problem solving was at a remarkably high level, this being both inherent and sustained by his environment.

On the Vernon Warden Reading Comprehension Test B he reached the level of 16 years. As this test was not timed, Alexander was able to use his contextual skills and reasoning to work out the correct response. He was unable to write at speed, and although his spelling (like his reading) had improved, it was still seen as being considerably below expectation based on age, ability and educational background.

Mr Freeland understood that Alexander's dyslexic problems were a source of frustration to him, and that if he only functioned within their limitations the resulting demoralisation could be very damaging. He commented:

> 'It is clearly crucial that such an exceptionally able and talented pupil's learning difficulties should be appropriately managed so as to cause the least impediment in the development of his talents and his overall learning so as to cause him the minimum of unnecessary frustration and threat to his self-esteem.'

To this end Mr Freeland made a thorough list of implications, which included the need to correct his very strained posture when writing; the advisability of reassessment by an occupational therapist for help with gross and fine motor development; and Alexander needed to improve his skills of written communication by two hours a week of specialist tuition through instrumental enrichment. He also recommended that Alexander should be given every possibility to bypass these difficulties through alternative means of communication. He was very enthusiastic about the possibility of his acquiring the skills to use a lap top computer to avoid recourse to pen and paper, which clearly inhibited the development of his ideas.

It was seen as crucial that all his teachers were aware of the nature and the cause of his difficulties, for it couldn't be stressed too heavily how important their understanding was for his progress. Mr Freeland strongly recommended that Alexander should not be penalised for his slowness in writing and that whatever form of modification was necessary, it should be implemented to compensate for his shortcomings.

Mr Freeland then addressed the vital issue of the 'A' level. He wrote:

> 'Alex is planning to undertake 'A' level English Literature which would be examined via 50 per cent course work. I probed with Alex his motivation for this and it appears to me that he is intrinsically motivated to undertake 'A' level English Literature while at the same time being aware that such an undertaking would be a source of pleasure to his parents. Given that Alex is predominantly intrinsically motivated for this, provided it fits in with the other studies I can see no reason why this should not act as yet a further boost to his self-esteem and a development of intrinsic interest. While the predominant theme with gifted children is to enrich their curriculum intake rather than to express them through I think that in Alex's case, sitting 'A' levels could be seen very simply as a form of structured enrichment.
>
> It would be very important that Alex was granted concessions at external examinations. I would

recommend that Alex use a tape recorder with a transcript provided for the Examiner. The advantage of this is that Alex has experience using a tape and this allows him to develop his ideas with reasonable speed.'

We were delighted with this assessment, for Mr Freeland clearly had not just the appropriate skills for his profession, but the insight to understand the true needs, emotionally as well as physically, of a child with an unusual combination of disability and exceptional ability, the very nature of the former locking the intellectual talent into a frustrated mind unless, though a combination of methods and approaches, it could be liberated.

I cannot over-emphasise how important I think it is for people of any age to undergo assessment if there is the possibility of dyslexia. In this area, knowledge is an enabling power: ignorance a prison of fear. I have come across several students who have the symptoms of dyslexia, but are afraid to be tested and 'labelled': I have met others who, through being diagnosed, have come to understand their difference and know there is both a reason for what they can't do, and recognised ways available for them to achieve goals previously thought beyond their wildest dreams.

We had learnt from GCSE that with such a peculiar case as Alexander's it is necessary to cover everything thoroughly – to dot every 'i' and cross every 't' – when dealing with the administration and presenting his case. We had felt that as the GCSE board had accepted his working method, the 'A' level board probably would as well, at least for the course work component. The problem was with the examination element. Would they understand enough to let him work on tape in the examination room? For although he had attained a degree of technical accomplishment on the typewriter, it was obvious that it in no way solved the problem of the effective recording of the quality of his ideas, as he did not communicate properly onto paper, only onto tape. When he tried to type work, the 17 words a minute were lost as the speed of his ideas clashed head on with his mind trying to control his hands. The result was that the ideas were curtailed, and the spelling truly dreadful.

We were aware that the standard concession for dyslexia in examinations was to grant 25 per cent extra time, but we knew that this, whilst being desirable to allow him to get through large chunks of text, especially in the critical appreciation paper, would in no way remedy his inability to record his complex ideas on paper.

By early December, Mrs Wade had enough documentation to approach the examination board through the college's examinations' office. She explained that Alexander was a flexi student at Fareham College studying for AEB 660 English Literature. She enclosed copies of the orthoptist's report, Mr Freeland's latest assessment, and a sample in the form of *The Eagle* (in Alexander's handwriting and in typescript for clarification purposes). She explained that his severe dyslexia and visual difficulties made it impossible for him to communicate his ideas in writing effectively for four main reasons: he could not think on to paper; he worked at a very slow speed; the final product was largely illegible; and his spelling was so bizarre that generally only those who knew him could guess at his meaning. She therefore asked if his normal method of working – tape and transcript – could be permitted in the 1994 summer unseen examination.

The six weeks it took the reply to arrive were real nail biting material. We knew that if he were made to write in the examination the outcome would be jeopardised, but we had clearly sent enough material for the board to be fully informed – for the response was favourable. He could use the tape and transcript method both for course work and in the final written papers. There was also a request for some material to be included in his own hand, with a transcript. Because of the extremely unusual nature of the case the board wished to refer the final assessment of the whole of work to senior examiners and moderators.

It was an enormous relief to have the worry lifted from our shoulders. Although we were confident of his ability, the question all along had been the method of presentation. There were still a couple of points that needed clarification – it was vital that the distress suffered by Alexander spending hours writing out something which he had initially enjoyed composing, was not repeated. So Mrs Wade asked if such handwritten material to be included could be limited to his original poetry, which would be short.

The other point that needed to be explained was that for the course work essays, the final version would not be the same as the original tape, as several drafts would be involved, but that all intermediate drafts containing his corrections could be included in the file. The board was pleased that all was being explained, and with everyone fully informed, teaching progressed at a steady pace.

However, school continued a black hole for Alexander: the more of him that was sucked in, the less could be seen of his true talents. Break times were still spent writing out spellings, and in addition his new English teacher had given him handwriting exercises. He hated these but we assured him that as it had been done with the best of intentions, he would have to learn diplomacy and humour the school by doing them.

In spite of several conversations between Andrew and the headmaster, the bullying persisted; Alexander frequently came home with ghastly accounts of what had happened to him in the toilets and changing rooms. I often felt, as I had done that first time when he told me of the boys sitting on his head, a sense of guilt that I was letting him down. This was, however, coupled with an awareness that we had made the situation known and that any further intervention would put Andrew in an awkward position.

Mr Freeland's report had emphasised his view that Alexander ought to have specialist teaching for reading and writing skills primarily aimed at improving hand–eye coordination on paper. He thought that this would ideally be provided in his own school setting, for, given the prevalence of dyslexia, it would be communicating a message that it is perfectly 'normal' to have learning difficulties. Mr Freeland recommended a local teacher with the appropriate skills. She agreed and we approached the headmaster, who allowed the same arrangements as the pre-prep – that the lessons would take place at lunch time.

I was grateful for this because I had been concerned that he might adopt the same policy as the headmaster of the upper school who, while permitting music lessons to take place on site in school time, refused the same possibility to dyslexics. Music, however delightful, is the icing on the cake, whereas the ability to communicate is the real bread and butter of existence.

The lessons were intriguing, the teaching professional and thorough, but after a while we felt it right to discontinue them because, from our point of view, they were not the way forward for Alexander, although no doubt they would be for others. My father was paying and I felt bad because I didn't want to continue the lessons when I didn't actually feel that they would effect a long term tangible alteration in the structure of Alexander's mind in the same way, for example,

as listening to Milton's *Paradise Lost* would. Here, as in all
options available, it is essential for parents to enable their
children to find the most appropriate way of communicating,
so that the disability of dyslexia is either minimised, as far
as possible through training, or bypassed by finding alternative methods of presentation. Our choice from this point
onwards was to concentrate exclusively on the latter.

Alexander's lower sixth course work year was a fairly
relaxed one. We studied one book each half term: *The
Elizabethan Poets* and *The Tempest* in the autumn; *Paradise Lost
Books I and II* and *The Catcher in the Rye* in the spring; *Notes
from the Rainforest* and *Our Mutual Friend* in the summer with
an extended essay on the *carpe diem* (seize the day) theme in
the (summer) holidays.

It was impossible for Mrs Wade to cover all the ground
in one hour a week, so Andrew and I, working in close
consultation with her, shared the teaching of all the texts. I
taught two-thirds of them as the burden of making the
transcripts fell entirely on Andrew's shoulders.

Mrs Wade helped enormously in drumming into Alexander the importance of a clear structure in his essays and
covered aspects of the texts that she considered could benefit
him through in-depth investigation. Psychologically her
input was important in that it provided an objectivity for
Alexander which could be overlooked when we were teaching him. It's often easy to disregard what your parents say
in the same way as you dismiss their instructions to tidy your
bedroom, but if someone else reinforces the viewpoint you
stop and take note.

About four hours in total each weekend were spent in
teaching him, which is probably about right, as a class of
students sharing the teacher's attention receives approxi-
mately five hours of class time per subject. As far as possible,

we made the materials available for him to listen to on tape at the same time as he read them, although we couldn't find audio versions of either *The Catcher in the Rye* or *Our Mutual Friend*. The latter proved a mammoth task but one which was planned and paced to make it possible. He read, or sometimes we read to him, one chapter a night for two months before we studied the text. The experience of a full length Dickens novel proved invaluable because Alexander learned so much about technique, style, themes and character presentation, all of which enriched his understanding of literature and human psychology. He found the portrayal of Bradley Headstone's self-consuming obsessive passion, and consequent mental breakdown gripping, as he traced the stages of disintegration through the different techniques of dialogue, description and analysis by Dickens. The book provided a stimulus to his thinking which was long term – only the other day there was an item on the news about confidence tricksters which Alexander immediately related to the Lammles, who deceived both society and, ironically each other, as to their wealth and status. His study of literature became increasingly important not just as a means of passing an examination, but of finding out about the complexities of the workings of the human mind as explored by some of the best thinkers of all time.

I became progressively worried during this year about the effect the English teaching at his school might have on his 'A' level studies. In order to encourage the children to read on a regular basis, the school had a book review system for the top two years. A book was chosen for analysis from a different category each half term. Marks were awarded both for the written text and for a picture illustrating some part of the story. We negotiated and were allowed to present Alexander's in a typed version.

He found it fun to pick from books as diverse as *The Time Machine* and *Matilda*, applying the same analytical techniques to each text. His commentaries were given due credit, and in spite of his drawings, generally good marks, but a worrying note was always present in the teacher's comments that Alexander was not telling the story. The review had to be divided into four sections: summary, characters, incidents and quotations. Alexander, in the summary section, gave an accurate and pithy account of the flavour and direction of the book, without going into an elaborate blow by blow recitation of what happened next. At home we had taught him never to tell the story in an essay, as the narrative approach is the sign of a very weak and pedestrian candidate.

I was worried that all the good work done by Mrs Wade on essay writing could be undermined, if on some level he actually came to believe that story telling was the right approach. There was no point in doing battle with the school on this matter, as I did not want to criticise their teaching of nine- to eleven-year-olds – I just didn't want it to have a detrimental effect on his mind. After a discussion with Alexander, we came to the conclusion that he should do the whole of the next year's book reviews during a week of his summer holiday in 1993. This would be beneficial in two respects: it would both provide more free time in half terms and holidays for 'A' level work and remove the pressure on him to change his approach to literature during his vital second year. This decision saved Alexander from self-doubt as the marks for the book reviews decreased the nearer to 'A' level he got.

Alexander has great interest in his Hungarian roots and had for some time maintained a correspondence, dictated or on tape, with his grandfather there whom he had not seen since he was five years old. He would write to him about the political affairs of the day and relate them to historical precedents.

That summer we arranged the most enormous surprise – Andrew and I took him to meet his grandfather. Emily we left for an adventure-packed week with my parents. We didn't take her for several reasons: at the age of six we felt that she was too young to enjoy what a sweltering 40°C capital city had to offer in mid-summer. Rather more significantly she had recently developed extrinsic asthma. In the oppressive heat the pollution is truly intolerable.

Alexander had no idea that he and I were to accompany Andrew, who had been going over to Hungary regularly since his father's return from exile. On the day of departure, Alexander asked if he could come and see the plane off and was pleased when we agreed: in fact, he was playing right into our hands. It wasn't until we were actually at the airport that he realised what was happening. His joy kept him buoyant throughout the flight.

We stayed with Andrew's aunt Magda, but only hours after our arrival György Faludy came to claim his grandson. To everyone's delight they were immediately immersed, not in pleasant chit chat about the journey but in a comparison of theories about the origin of the universe! Each day we would deliver Alexander to his grandfather and collect him in the evening. Left to their own devices, the pair would explore the museums and art galleries of Budapest, chat in coffee houses or wander by the Danube, while we enjoyed the unexpected freedom, in which all we had to do was to entertain ourselves, knowing that the children were both perfectly happy. It was the first time since their birth that we had been free to spend time doing whatever we wanted.

The trip was even better for Alexander than the brief visit to Eurodisney had been the previous year: it introduced him to a new culture that he felt part of; it cemented a bond with his other grandfather and introduced him to distant relatives who made a great fuss of him. In addition, in his grandfather's care, he developed an unhealthy taste for coffee so strong that the very smell engenders giddiness.

With the course work file complete by the beginning of the autumn term, final moderation was conducted by the Head of English at Fareham College, Graeme Hodgson, whose open-mindedness in relation to such a young candidate in his department was indicative of his enlightened, but academically rigorous approach. The work in the file was of the the standard we had expected – starting with a preponderance of 'C' grades when he was still nine, and progressing to firm 'B's by the time he was ten and a half. On balance, though, it averaged a 'C', which was really all we could have hoped for by doing the course work in the first year.

We were now ready to embark on the examination texts. Far more work than I could have imagined went into this second year, as Alexander had to be taught to get things right first time round on tape. This meant that, from the first weekend, he taped a timed essay each week. This, of course, had to be transcribed, evaluated and discussed with him.

The course was 'open book', which meant that students could bring their annotated texts into the examination room with them. The type of question asked was therefore very different from in my own schooldays when we learned numerous quotations by heart. Quite other, rather advanced analytical skills are called for from today's pupils. Seeing what Alexander had done to his copy of *Our Mutual Friend* when studying it, I was aware that his annotations were illegible not only to me, but after a while to him as well, and they actually obscured the text. The mirror-reversing of his cross references also made it impossible for him to locate key passages.

The examination board therefore had to be approached again, to ask permission for his comments to be copied into his books so that they were legible. In any event, I felt it was vital that everything we did was, and was seen to be, open and above board. Permission was granted, but of course this meant even more work, just so Alexander could function like the other students.

We made a rough calculation that in this second year, together with detailed preparation aimed at his individual needs, teaching (which by then took about six hours a weekend), transcribing and going over his work with him, we spent about fifteen hours a week on his 'A' level. Emily's patience during this time is truly to be commended.

He was happier at school this year in one respect, for having progressed to the Uppers (the final year of the lower school), there were fewer people left to bully him. Unfortunately, though, his friend had gone up to the next part of the school and he had no one to identify with. Being made a library monitor had a positive impact on Alexander's life at school, for it meant he could take refuge there much of the time, out of the reach of the playground bullies. Alexander was fond of his English teacher, who respected his intellect and commented in his reports on his astute and intelligent answers to comprehension exercises. He praised his keen awareness of figurative language as well as his leading role in class discussions.

We worked through the examination texts at the same pace of a book each half term, starting with *Tess of the d'Urbervilles*, then *Antony and Cleopatra* followed by *She Stoops to Conquer* and *The Metaphysical Poets* (Donne, Herbert, Marvell and Carew). On top of this, he had to be introduced to the unseen critical appreciation paper and the skills involved in responding to the exact demands of the questions. We arranged for him to sit a mock examination at the end of the spring term – this was almost as much for the college's benefit as his own, so it could work out what was needed and how it was to be administered. Mrs Wade had been practising transcription of his essays, but was not as quick as Andrew had become, so the experience of having to type out two whole examination papers was also valuable for her. Alexander was given a room of his own with the invigilator sitting unobtrusively at the back, and he had to get used to the presence of another person as he worked aloud – which is something I'm sure I would feel quite self-conscious about. It's not a problem writing while another person is in the room, but I wouldn't like to talk my answers in front of someone.

The mock revealed very substantial signs of intellectual development in Alexander and he got a 'B' in it. This seemed to act as some sort of catalyst. It showed him that he could do it, and the way his work took off between Easter and the examination was really astonishing. He developed an overview, a genuine understanding and a maturity that surprised even us, particularly in his responses to unseen pieces where he reached beneath the surface of complex ideas and positively enjoyed the intellectual process of unravelling both *how* they worked, technically and stylistically, and the emotions, experiences and ideas which had led to their composition.

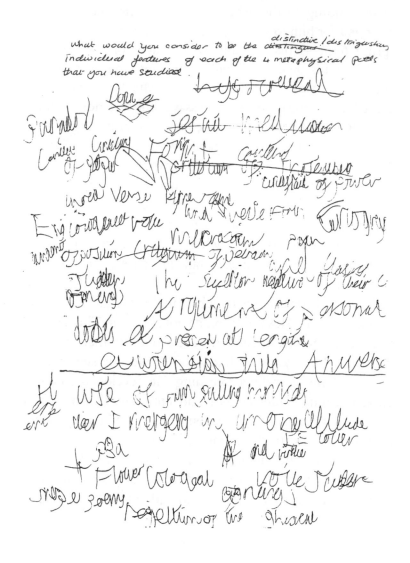

Figure 3 Alexander's handwritten plan for an essay

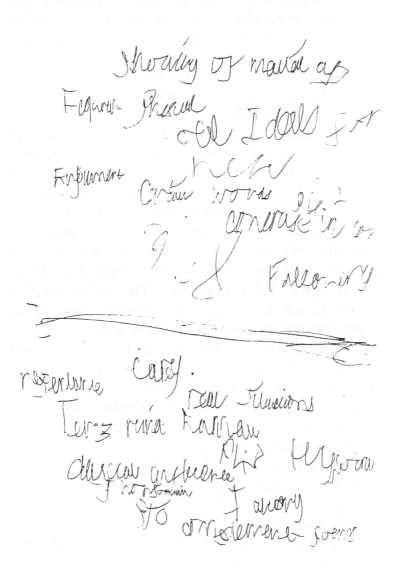

Figure 3 Alexander's handwritten plan for an essay (continued)

Timed essays became a challenge and an amusement – he was getting better all the time – in fact on the day before the actual examination he did an essay on the metaphysical poets, which as far as I could make out scored more than full marks. I knew we were there and that if he did as well on the day he could score an 'A', and bring his 'C' at course work up to a 'B' overall.

I have included the plan of this essay to show what his writing was like when he was actually thinking, rather than just copying something out. The plan represented what he had composed in his mind, and the dictation had to proceed swiftly, while he could still read what he had written.

We asked, and were grateful for, the cooperation of Alexander's headmaster regarding not only his absence from school for the examinations, but also in the delicate matter of keeping the whole business quiet. The very last thing we wanted was for his contemporaries to become aware of the impending examination and to worry or tease him about it.

The critical appreciation paper came first and all seemed to have gone well. There followed a two-week wait for the set texts paper. In the lull Andrew took him to see *She Stoops to Conquer* at Christ's Hospital School theatre. We've always tried to make texts available to him in as many ways as possible. Alexander enjoys the theatre and particularly the quaint ambience of Christ's Hospital with the boys and girls in their black knickerbockers, mustard socks and flowing black gowns.

A far more important and personal reason for visiting Christ's Hospital is that our friends, Andrew and Clare Phillips and their children, Clifford, Matthew, Amelia (our god-daughter) and Henry (born a few weeks ago) live there. The two Andrews have known each other since the age of nine – over thirty years; Alexander and Clifford have been friendly since they were both quite small. Through all the difficult phases chronicled in this book, Andrew and Clare have been a source of constant encouragement. We have always been secure in the knowledge that when things became really difficult, we could turn to them for good advice, and a fresh, reassuring perspective.

I waited nervously for Alexander to emerge from the final examination, but from what he told me, I at least gathered that he had passed! On the way home we stopped at Sainsbury where I told him he could have what he wanted. He chose French bread, mushrooms, a *Sister Act* video, strawberries and a bottle of Spanish Cava – well, he deserved it!

It was over for him, but not for Elisabeth Wade. I later found out that it took her two whole days to transcribe the answers.

Alexander's Account:

Winter term 1992 to Summer term 1993 – my second year in the lower school and my first year of ' A' level

Things were a little easier when I did the 'A' level. My parents were able to get the lower school to allow me to be permanently 'excused' from Saturday sport, one of the school's little idiosyncrasies. This took off one of the pressures that I had been under while doing the GCSE. Also, I only had to work two hours each day at the weekend and saw my tutor – Mrs Wade – once a week. My work became part of family life. There was a routine. My mother and I would go and work in the study, while my sister drew at her desk in the living room, watched a video – her favourites being *Alice in Wonderland* and *The Beauty and the Beast*, or played with my father, progressing from *My Little Pony* to *Risk* over the two year period.

My early work was concerned with the Elizabethan poets and as background material, *The Elizabethan World Picture*. The Elizabethans believed that there was a hierarchy of life, starting at the bottom with inanimate objects like boulders, and progressing through living things such as trees, through sentient animals to human beings, and ultimately to angels and God. My study of these involved writing essays about how the Elizabethan poets were relevant to the modern day, and how human experience does not alter dramatically, and that the things we are scared of now such as death, were current topics in times before, in the poetry of men like Shakespeare and Spenser, as was the desire for some sort of immortality – for example, 'One day I wrote her name upon the strand'.

My reading of Dickens' *Our Mutual Friend* later in the year introduced me, amongst other things, to the world of social satire. In particular I enjoyed the Veneerings, who had varnished over their mysterious origins to present a polished and rather artificial exterior, until eventually the carefully constructed image shattered.

However, my real academic studies were not the only dominating factor at that time in my life. There was a constant conflict between what I was learning at home and what I was doing at school generated by the great intellectual gap between the two.

For instance, at home I was told 'not to tell the story' but to 'analyse'. At school we were told to tell the story, draw pictures, and make basic observations about the text, such as whether a character changed at all during the story. I thought that using the things I had learned at home would serve me well, but this was not so. I was confused whether to follow the technique prescribed by my English teacher or my parents. It was easy to criticise in the safety of my own home, but it was a different matter at school where I was forced to agree verbally with everything the teacher said, as are all school children of that age.

An important event concerning this springs to mind. We were given an exercise in class to write a letter to a relative, in the nature of a thank you for a book by Hans Christian Andersen which the teacher gave us an accurate description of: it had a leather binding, and if I remember correctly, gold edging. I thought that as well as describing the book, I should also discuss some of the influences in Andersen's work from his life which I had learned about from watching television. I thought that my reference to Andersen's life, and the way I had backed it up, could be seen as in a small way taking the initiative, and also as a sign of some sort of appreciation of the work itself. I was told that it was silly, and that you don't put that sort of thing in letters. The teacher then asked me rhetorically if I would put such a thing in a letter. The only reply I could make was, of course, 'no', even though I would personally do so. I felt as if I did want to contradict her, but I knew I couldn't.

Another difficulty at school was again the spelling and handwriting. I was made to copy down and trace correct letters from passages in an old book, which I have to say was not designed for dyslexics, that edition being published in, I think, 1947, before people actually recognised dyslexia! I would often get remarks from my geography teacher, who was particularly non-understanding about my handwriting, concerning how I could do it so well for my English teacher and not for him, as he saw it. But there is a difference between copy book writing where all you have to do is concentrate on the act of transcribing, and work where your brain is supposed to be thinking of a topic, and not of what your hands are doing.

The bullying did not go away during my second year in the lower school and in some ways got worse. There were several very unpleasant incidents which to some extent affect me now. One of these, which illustrates the type of things that were going on at the time, occurred during a ritual which was carried out by the boys in my year group and some others. The aim was to impersonate homosexuals by doing what the boys thought homosexuals did, that was, grabbing hold of each others' genitalia.

On one occasion when I was coming back from my lunch in the playground, a group of boys from my class approached, led by a boy who often threw my personal property around the class room, but had never done anything physical to me previously. He drew his hand back, and punched me straight in my testicles. I doubled up and stumbled back a few paces, while they moved off at a leisurely pace, as if this was a run of the mill thing, and nothing had happened.

My stomach felt very empty, in a way as if I had thrown up, and as soon as I took my lunch box back into the class room, I looked around for a member of staff. It wasn't that I was scared of an immediate repetition, but it had shaken me up, both because of the physical pain and the unexpected nature of the attack. I was fortunate, as I then thought it, to stumble across the headmaster, and I told him about the incident. The boys were told off, but nothing was *done*, and they started to tease me about the incident later, and chanted names at me, as they often did, such as 'tell tale tit' in a high pitched juvenile monotone, which was their way of getting their own back on me.

Another constant problem for me was the bullying which occurred in the changing rooms on the two afternoons a week which we had on the school playing fields. In the previous year I had been bullied there, so I decided that I should, as often as possible, go into corners where few people were about. However, this worsened the situation, since when they did come at me, I could not escape. The actual bullying involved punching me, kicking me and throwing me down on the floor. My feelings were odd because I was the centre of attention, but in a way which I hated: the only way I could be part of their minds was when they were kicking me. This made me feel very dejected. All I was good for from their point of view was being their practice football. In a strange way, I hoped that they would hurt me badly enough for something to be done about it, so the torment would stop. It was a hope which I half hid from myself, and even now am only beginning to understand.

They would fling my kit about the changing room so that on other occasions when I was asked why I had not got the appropriate articles, I would have to reply that I had lost them. This made me feel humiliated in front of everyone else and got me into trouble with the teachers: fines had to be paid to retrieve articles from lost property.

But where were the supervising staff? Well, there weren't any. The teachers popped into the changing rooms occasionally to see whether every one was ready or not before the game started, and returned valuables and watched the changing for a brief time after the games were over. My father complained about this to the school and the headmaster made an announcement in assembly. However, the incidents did not stop, and nothing was *done*, and my kit continued to be thrown about.

I was also teased because I could not match the other pupils' academic standards, because I was always in the last Maths set, because I couldn't catch a ball, because I couldn't draw a map properly, because I couldn't make two compasses make a perfect circle. I remember one boy saying to me in a knowing way, 'I know how you did your GCSE. I've got it all figured out', implying that it wasn't my own work. I strongly suspect my academic problems at the school to be the cause for such remarks. However, this time I knew I wasn't stupid, because I had discovered that I conformed to a standard different from theirs which they could not appreciate. I began to rationalise their behaviour, to try and understand the causes behind it. I strongly suspect that a certain jealousy may have been one motive; personal circumstances were another. The boy who claimed that he knew how my GCSE had been done, himself alienated other children by boasting about his sailing prowess. I came to the conclusion that I was not the one with the problem. I realised that I could not be blamed for my own personal disadvantages, and that my personality and limitations were not the product of my own choice.

+++++

The second year of 'A' level and the last year of the lower school

The next stage of my history began in the summer holidays of 1993 with a visit to the Hungarian republic where my father was born and where my grandfather lives, along with all the rest of my family on my father's side. I didn't actually know that I was going, but, as my parents observed at the time, I was rather gullible. For instance, I didn't see the suspicious side of why my father was taking three suitcases with him, and why we were having the water and electricity shut off for a week. My mother told me it was because we would be out most of the time and would doing loads of fun things; neither did I see why it was so important that my sister should be sent to my grandparents the day before my father was scheduled to leave.

The night before leaving, my parents told me that I would have to get up early the next morning because my mother wanted us to all have breakfast at the same time to save her making it again later. The next morning my parents called me into their bedroom. My mother said that as I had asked so nicely, we were going to be able to go to the airport with my father to see him off. I was very excited at this, since I had never been to an airport before. At that moment I had a twinge of suspicion and asked if I was coming too. My parents told me that of course I wasn't. At the airport I got another twinge of suspicion when my father was handing over the tickets, since my mother told me to look away and said: 'Is there someone you recognise up there?' I looked searchingly but could find no one, so I turned round and we were able to go on. My father took three passports out of his pocket and shuffled them. At this point I guessed, and with elation, cried: 'Yes! Oh, thank you very much!'. Then my mother was very cross with my father and said, 'You've gone and given it away'. I was told that we were going for just a week and that I would be able to see my grandfather while we were there. I also found out that they hadn't intended to tell me until we got onto the plane.

In Budapest I was able to see all the relatives that I had only heard about for years. I spent a lot of time with my grandfather. We would make our way out by tram and by bus to his flat in the suburbs. As well as eating a great deal of rice and mushrooms with green and red peppers, salt and butter added, we had very long conversations on topics ranging from Queen Elizabeth of Hungary to the Hungarian Revolution of 1848, and from that, the Hungarian apple market of 1955. How did this happen? Well, my grandfather said so many things which I didn't understand, I had to ask him a series of questions to try and understand the briefest sentence, and after I had done so, there were more questions to be asked about his reply, so that we deviated from the original subject so much that I couldn't remember what I was talking to him about in the first place. However, this was an educational experience which led me to understand the reasons for subjects as different as why Henry VIII was refused a divorce from Catherine of Aragon, by the Pope that is, because her nephew was occupying Rome at the time, and how Hungarian peasants managed to cheat the communist party.

My curiosity about the meaning of art, and the different interpretations that can be placed on paintings was increased when my grandfather took me on a visit to the beautiful art gallery in the old city of Buda, known as the Vár, in the former royal palace. Though some of the paintings depict self-indulgently patriotic scenes from Hungarian history, scenes which only a Hungarian could love, I was able to start to see how symbolism operated in painting and how art developed from the crudest of medieval altarpieces to the finest of portraits and scenes of the eighteenth and nineteenth centuries. This was something which was to serve me in good stead, and encourage me in what has now become a very great fascination for me, that is, the study of art history. This I feel is now an essential part of my personality, and is how I like to spend my spare time when my father takes me to London to look at the National Gallery and other museums.

After I had returned from Budapest, there was work to be done. As well as having my extended essay to write, my parents advised me to compose all the book reviews for the following year, so that more time could be left for my 'A' level and to prevent me from being torn by the different demands of the two. I tried to apply what I had learned at 'A' level to the book reviews as nearly as possible, and make them intellectually alive. I was to have a new teacher for English who I thought would appreciate such an effort. I was right to think that he liked it, but the problems with story telling remained. For instance, in my review of H.G. Wells's *The Time Machine*, I wrote as my summary:

> 'In the book, H.G. Wells gives the more modern view of the four dimensions, to the Time Traveller, who puts it before a sceptical nineteenth century audience whose hardened lives and careers put a barrier of practicality up against the Time Traveller's extra-

ordinary theories. It follows the Time Traveller's extraordinary accounts of the surprising future to which the human race is supposed to be destined.'

I thought this to be a fair and rational summary, but at the end of the review, my teacher said that although I had made some interesting observations, rather more was still needed in the form of a summary. My mother warned me not to tell my teacher that I'd done them all in the summer holiday, as he might make me do them again. I was very pleased to be able to get all the book reviews done, since it helped me put them in perspective and not worry about the comments on this aspect of my work.

In my final year, my English teacher, who was also my form teacher, was very kind to me. In his lessons he allowed me to shine, and let me explain poetry and devices which I had heard of, such as irony, rhyme scheme and personification, my knowledge of which he seemed very impressed with. This made me feel very happy and gave me some self-confidence. It was quite a change from the attitude which had greeted me in the previous two years. He accepted that I had problems, and urged me to continue with my handwriting practice, but understood when I found things difficult, and tried to help me with my spelling, not by covering each sheet of paper with red marks, which had depressed me for several years, but by pointing out the main things that were wrong and how they could be corrected in a manner which was not patronising and was not intended to lower my confidence in the way I did things.

My form teacher was also the school librarian and chose me as one of his assistants. This meant I gave up my break time and lunch time once a week, but in reality I took over many other people's shifts because I wanted to stay in the library. This was for several reasons: the first was that I enjoyed myself in there and had spent much time in the library in the preceding two years; the second, and probably most important, was that it seemed a safe haven from the bullies for me as it was seen as my home territory. It gave me a modicum of respect which was something new and made me very happy, since I had not enjoyed it before in any field for a sustained period. The congratulations that had greeted my GCSE lasted for two weeks before the open and friendly hands clenched themselves into menacing fists.

However, my soupçon of respect did not stop the bullying, and now the focus was more than ever on sport. For instance, on one occasion we had been told to take a tennis racket and hit a ball against the wall. There was plenty of space and I was in no-one's way, but I was constantly shoved to the back, punched and kicked. Rackets and balls were swung at me and hit me, mysteriously but, it was claimed, accidentally. This was accompanied by name calling and I ended up in tears. The PE teacher reprimanded them, but this brought the usual repercussions later for me.

These were not the only circumstances under which they would take the opportunity to tease me. On occasions I would be able to pluck the prized yellow sphere from the air during a rounders' match, but more often it would go straight past me, or hit me in the stomach. This gave rise to the allegation by one boy that I seemed to turn my dyslexia on and off. He said this sarcastically, as if to imply that my disabilities were not genuine and I found such an attitude of doubt particularly hurtful.

Teasing also occurred in the changing room where one boy, a rugby fanatic, and a few others took up the cry by chanting: 'This is an impression of you. Oh, I can't get a ball. I'm dyslexic.' Or 'Ooh, I've fallen over. I must be dyslexic.' This taunting continued in the playground, which is why I took flight to the library so often, but not even that was a permanent sanctuary. For instance, one boy would dance around on the tables or come to the librarian's desk where I would be seated, and stand in the way, stopping other children getting their books stamped, while taunting me about my disabilities and other things, such as why I was always going to the teachers to stop the bullying.

On one occasion when I was very upset, and as far as I can remember, crying, he grabbed hold of me under the chin and pulled my skin right down. I thought I had to show strength by not weeping any more, and that by not crying out, he might take that as a hint to leave me alone, but he did not. A friend of mine fetched a member of staff but the bully made some excuses along the lines that I was picking on him by asking him to leave the library, and that I had blown things out of proportion. The member of staff said that he had a fair idea of what was going on and told us to stay away from each other, which was a very tactful thing to do, because I suppose if he had apportioned much more blame, he'd have made things more difficult for me, since it would have brought repercussions. The bullying seemed in some ways worse that year, since I had no longer my friend as a companion, because he had gone up to the next part of the school.

This year, I developed the technique of the timed essay at home, in practice for the examination. I was very afraid to begin with, because I never thought I'd be able to finish them on time, but I did get better, and my essays got longer, so that from the 80 rotations [on the counter of the tape recorder] that I would produce in the early days, I would progress to 150 or more, and would advance from a mid-

dling 'C' to a comfortable 'B' or 'A', as we reckoned it, since
these essays were not submitted as course work and reviewed
only by Mrs Wade and ourselves.

The mock examination took place before Easter. I remember the day well: I wore my favourite jumper, and was
pleasantly surprised at one of the questions, which was
related to the *Horatian Ode*, a metaphysical poem which I
had recently studied. I enjoyed writing the essay, but was
relieved when it was over. My performance in the mock exam
gave me succour, and made me feel confident and less
daunted about the real one which was to take place during
the summer term.

The next important stage relating to my 'A' level was the
half term I spent doing old papers to prepare me for the real
examination. This was where I really began to develop my
ideas. My favourite essay at this time was concerning a poem
about grief. I was asked to explore the ways in which William
Jay Smith presented his thoughts and feelings in *Elegy, For
Bateman Edwards, d. 1 Sept. 1947* and how he transmitted those
feelings to the reader. The recurring idea in this poem was
of mirrors used to explore the complexity of the human mind
in encountering the absence of a loved one. Smith personi-
fied his fears into dragons to mirror the spiritual torment he
underwent and to give us an indication of the terrors that he
faced:

> The world that evening was a world of mirrors
> Where two great dragons from opposing caves,
> Mirror their eyes and mirror all the scales...

I'll quote briefly from my essay here: 'There is the idea that
the poet has lost all identity. I feel that it is another aspect
of the two mirror image, since the poet has no individual
character now, but has temporarily joined the rank and file

of those who grieve. He is a mere reflection of the other mirror on the wall, since the two mirrors face each other, and reflect back the image of each other, just like the poet and his friend's memory reflect back the thoughts of the friend when he was alive.'

Although this essay was written to help me practise exam technique, I enjoyed the material in its own right, for it enabled me to explore an emotion that I couldn't envisage from my own experience. My results from this preparatory work made me feel ready and sure of myself, so that when the time for the first exam came, as I remember it, on the day of the El Alamein commemorations, I wasn't scared. I decided that I should try hard, but felt that it was just another essay.

But the day of the second exam, two weeks after the first, is the one I like to remember most. It also happened to be the first day of Wimbledon. After the exams were over, my mother took me down to Sainsburys where I bought a *Sister Act* video, four baguettes and a bottle of third rate and very bad Spanish Cava (unfortunately my mother bought a second bottle so we could get £2 off). That night, between us all, we drank half of the first bottle, mixing it with elderflower to make it palatable. I didn't feel the weight drifting from my shoulders until a couple of weeks later, at the end of term.

On the last day of term I felt immeasurably happy. Three years of torment were coming to an end. At that time I was full of apprehension as to what my 'A' level result would be, but also greatly relieved and happy that the combined strain of academic work and athletic pressure were gone.

CHAPTER SIX

Being Unconventional

'A' level was over, but Alexander's education had only just begun. He had visited art galleries in Budapest, but had never been to any major ones in England. The first trips to London were fun in that they were explorations of new and exciting locations – museums and art galleries with tempting tea rooms and shops. This initial pleasure rapidly trans-formed itself into a passion. Andrew drove him to London most weekends, for standing in front of a painting and discussing it is now the single thing that gives Alexander the keenest pleasure.

Events to look forward to in particular are exhibitions and study days. During the last year he has been to: the Ashmolean Museum in Oxford; the Courtauld; the Victoria and Albert Museum; the National Gallery; the Tate; the Royal Academy and the Hayward. These regular opportu-nities to view works of art have sharpened Alexander's aesthetic appreciation to an acute point, and this, in combi-nation with the pre-existing intellectual structure obtained through 'A' level, has pushed Art History to the top of his agenda, as well as providing him with an enormous amount of entertainment.

Dr Dean, a close family friend, is also a favourite third party in these outings, and when Alexander returns from such a day he is bursting to recount details of the discussions that have excited him so. When he is on his own with Andrew it is not unusual for him to pause in front of a painting and talk about it for twenty minutes. However, with Dr Dean, a three way, vigorous debate is the more customary format, often occasioning curious glances from passers by at the strange spectacle of two men and a twelve-year-old in animated discussion.

The two years of 'A' level forged very close intellectual links between Alexander and me. I knew just how his mind functioned and how to make it work; he became familiar with my intellectual patterning as well. I felt that now the examinations were over, it would be healthy to allow some sort of distance to develop. I don't mean emotionally, because I think that, owing to his ability and desire to communicate from a very early age, I have been lucky in being able to understand him in a way that would not have been possible if he had had that rough and tumble protective coating so common in boys, and from understanding comes a special love. The distance I wanted was an intellectual one so that he didn't automatically look to me as a source of, or a sounding board for, his knowledge.

Alexander wanted to visit Budapest again, but our funds didn't stretch to a family outing. He therefore went with Andrew and returned on his own as an unaccompanied minor two weeks later. This was the first time he had been away from me in any real sense. He was not even going to be with Andrew and Aunt Magda – he was to stay at his grandfather's by himself with Andrew visiting each day. I think this experience of semi-independence did him a great deal of good.

By this time his grandfather had moved from his flat in the hills above the capital into a magnificent apartment overlooking the Danube. The nature of the arrangement was peculiarly Hungarian – he was given the palatial suite for his lifetime, and a part of it would eventually become a museum containing books and artefacts relating to his life. We were all very happy for him. From being a non-person for thirty years he had had more than a dozen books, reprints included, published since his return. Having been banned for so long, his poetry was now part of the national curriculum.

While they were away, I started a decorating campaign on the house which had been sorely neglected during the intense activity of the past three years. Emily developed a real joy in reading that summer, and one has only to look at her to see that, although in terms of stimulus we respond to our children's individual needs, we have not forced either of them down a particular path. He couldn't read, in the conventional sense: she loves it; he listens to the radio and to tapes: she has devoured numerous series such as *Mallory Towers*. Both children have grown up in the same environment, but there is no way you can compel an eight-year-old to read and enjoy *Othello*. What I am saying is that we have not *made* Alexander study these things. We merely gave him what he needed in the same way as Emily is constantly provided with paper, paint, glue, pencils and sellotape, as her favourite hobby is making things.

In addition to home improvements, my other tasks involved negotiations with Winchester College and the Open University. Although Alexander had always looked forward to entering the upper school, his experiences in the lower school had made him eager for us to follow up the contact we had made after GCSE. This, and the letter we had received from the headmaster of the upper school in February influenced us in our decision to explore other options. The letter had offered him a place for the following September, but I found it double edged in that it said that he preferred to leave the judgement about whether to accept the place to us and that the situation would have to be reviewed after two years. It made me feel very insecure, for it was clear that a question mark yet again hung over his progress through the school. It certainly made me feel justified in having followed the 'A' level programme with him, for how else would his abilities have been recognised?

Between the end of the exams and their trip abroad, Andrew and Alexander had gone for an informal interview with the head of English at Winchester, Mr Simon Taylor, who seemed very enthusiastic about the possibility of his coming that September. I was to write to the headmaster, Mr James Sabben-Clare and put the case formally. His reply was a great disappointment to us. He stated that the only route into the school for Alexander would be through the conventional means of entrance or scholarship exams which, he believed, judging from what he knew, Alexander would have great difficulty with. He went on to remark that the school was well used to dealing with boys of outstanding intellectual potential, so Winchester would have the flexibility to cater for Alexander's strengths; he did not, however, see how it could do the same for his weaknesses.

My father had long thought that the way forward for Alexander was to enrol for an Open University degree. Alexander himself had been listening to their programmes for years, often in the early mornings before the rest of us were awake. As 'A' level drew to a close, he too began asking if we could look into the possibility of his starting a degree – after all, it seemed the logical next step.

Andrew and I had discussed the possibility, and it seemed like a good option – we did not want to follow the example of a maths prodigy we had heard of some years earlier whose father had accompanied her to university when she had been about Alexander's age. We felt that the important thing was to keep him in the company of his contemporaries (even though he preferred the companionship of adults) and adapt his school timetable so that he could pursue a degree at the same time.

Andrew had written for all the documents, but when they came we noticed that, although there was no upper limit on age, applicants had to be at least eighteen. We had heard, though, of some children studying maths with the Open University – so we knew there was hope and, at the same time as the interview at Winchester, negotiations began. Letters were written and lengthy phone calls made. The people we dealt with even at this early stage in the process, before the 'A' level results had come out, were very open minded: it was just that the case was so unusual. The question was, how could an eleven-year-old have the emotional perception and maturity to handle the concepts involved in an arts degree? To be good at Maths at an early age is unusual, but not without precedent, but it had never been suggested that a child of Alexander's age could have the intellectual capacity necessary to handle arts subjects at this level.

It was a summer of waiting and anticipation. Andrew had returned a week before the 'A' level results and the tension mounted as the day drew nearer. Alexander was interviewed and photographed by the local paper the day before the results so that the news could make the early editions. The final photographs were marvellous, but the picture session was one of the most comic performances I have witnessed:

he was balanced in various poses on piles of encyclopaedias – he wobbled and fell off. The reporter crouched behind, trying to hold him on. Each time he was asked to raise his left hand, he lowered his right. Emily, who was most patient throughout, found his antics highly amusing.

Then came the interview with me, which has caused us all so much trouble since. Andrew was not present, as he is a magistrate and was sitting in court at the time. One of the questions I was asked was *why* we had gone in for all the exams in the first place. I tried to put the whole thing in context, and explained about Alexander's low self-esteem before we had had him tested for dyslexia, and how he had been bullied and called stupid. The exams were to give him his own identity – they were an externally verifiable measure of his intelligence.

The day itself dawned. Andrew told me not to worry as he had dreamed that Alexander had passed with a 'B'. I was at the college early, and, as before, telephoned home with the result – 'B'. It was what we had hoped for. There followed a hectic afternoon of photographic sessions with the national press this time, as well as actual interviews with the local television and radio stations. I was surprised at how controlled Alexander was in his responses and felt his measured answers to be indicative of the degree of maturity he had reached.

That evening he and Andrew appeared live on Meridian. I think it was more nerve racking for Emily and me watching at home than it was for them. One of the questions we had been constantly asked throughout these two days was – 'what next?' I had to tell Alexander not to talk about our hopes for the Open University, because I did not want to jeopardise his case by putting unfair media pressure on them for a decision.

We bought all the national papers the next day. He had made a big splash across the board. My favourite headline was from *The Times* because, in a virtual oxymoron, it summed up the unusual nature of his achievement: 'Dyslexic pupil 11, leads honours for 'A' levels.' After the newspapers and the cards came the letters of congratulation, from as far away as New Zealand, where a former colleague had spotted an article in his local paper, which had been fed the news through Reuters. We received letters offering advice too, but as these involved yet more tests, although we explored the possibilities, in the end we felt that enough was enough.

Other, quite desperate letters, came from the parents of dyslexics who had been given hope by Alexander's achievement and wanted to consult us about what they should do next. They talked of how they felt branded as pushy parents with unrealistic expectations. Some sought details about the method we had followed to liberate our son from the limitations imposed by his dyslexia. Others just wanted to talk – to tell their stories of frustration at the refusal of schools to take proper notice of their children's conditions. I replied to them all.

Although each one was different, the common theme in my advice was to persevere in fighting for their child – the first step being the dyslexic test, and the second, if the IQ was high enough, joining MENSA. That way they couldn't just be dismissed as parents with exaggerated expectations, for here was irrefutable proof of an intelligence locked inside a disability. The third step had to be researching all the options available in terms of remedial help and alternative methods of presentation. It is vital to have working practice established well in advance of examinations.

I stressed that the most important thing was to find out what their child *was* good at, and give him or her every opportunity to develop that talent, whether it be photography, football, music or model making, so that an identity could be established separate from the dyslexia. I believe that if a child can feel special in some way and have confidence in his or her ability in a particular field, then the frustrations experienced in the areas of spelling, reading and writing will not be allowed to become the sole focus of life and self-perception.

Alexander entered the upper school, and as with his GCSE achievement, his 'A' level success was not mentioned at the beginning of term assembly. Many people commented on its absence, but the lack of acknowledgement seemed to me to send a message to all who were expecting to hear it referred to, of the value the school placed on Alexander's hard work, dedication, and unique achievement.

A couple of days into term, the local paper rang to see if it could include Alexander in its 'A' level update supplement. It already had plenty of photos to choose from, so another interview in person would not be necessary, but what were his plans? I told the reporter that I couldn't comment, as I didn't want to talk about something that hadn't actually materialised yet. I said I would get back to him. I contacted the Open University which was just about to write with the official offer of a place: preparatory work would start in the autumn term and the actual degree course in February.

In the newspaper he was put under the covering headline of, and next to, the column detailing the school's examination results – but one day, while in the headmaster's waiting room, I browsed through the cuttings file left there for visitors to peruse. There was the page – but the article on Alexander had been removed. I was slightly hurt but, I suppose, not really surprised.

The real surprise came in a letter from the headmaster telling me that he had received written representations expressing considerable resentment concerning my comments in the press. I was invited for discussions, but was advised that it would be necessary at some stage in the future to consider quite carefully the implications of the press reports.

I was initially worried in case some veiled threat was present in that word 'implications', but decided that the whole affair should be treated positively. I was heartened by reports from friends who had been present at the previous year's prizegiving that, although they could not remember the whole of the headmaster's speech, what had most stuck in their minds was his pronouncement that a good school was one that did its best, when it was best, for each individual pupil. I thought this comment truly enlightened, and as the headmaster, although never having spoken to Alexander, had offered his congratulations in the letter, I felt that the forthcoming meeting would be an ideal opportunity to tell him about my son's needs as well as to answer his queries about the press report.

At the meeting, I asked if consideration could be given to letting Alexander pursue a 50 per cent timetable to allow him to study for a degree whilst staying in a school environment. I was cautiously optimistic with the response that he could see no problems in practice, but that as matters of principle were involved, the case would have to be put before the governors.

The topic of bullying arose, one of my concerns being that during Alexander's time at the school so far, there had been no official policy document on the matter. I only hope that when one comes into operation, it will make the lives of other children easier.

The objections to the press coverage seemed to be in how my observations had been interpreted, for the comments themselves had been unelaborated and not at all controversial. Indeed, I had been very restrained, having been careful not to criticise the school at all, or talk of the suggestions that we should educate him elsewhere; nor had I mentioned any insensitivity to his condition on the part of the staff. I was bewildered by the whole affair, as what I had said was not actually contentious. I could only assume that those who had known what Alexander had suffered had interpreted my comments as personal criticisms. Was this supposed to be the only school in the country where children were not taunted for being different?

The headmaster thought that the next step was for a meeting to be held for me to justify myself before all those who felt they had a grievance. The idea horrified me and I perceived it as totally counterproductive. I explained that my comments to the press had been very low key and had not detailed the misery that Alexander had suffered at the hands of bullies. As he had come through it alive, I wanted to treat it as past history rather than resurrecting old wounds. Indeed, there was so much that I hadn't said, and have not elaborated in this book, that I thought such a meeting would be for the purpose of *making* me say the things that I had not stated in public, and I was in no mood to be drawn into argument.

ITN got hold of Alexander's story and rang to see if they could interview him for a slot on their main news. They wanted to film him at school, but as this did not seem the best of ideas, I tactfully suggested that Fareham College might be a more appropriate location.

The college was very accommodating, making rooms available to the television crew. Both the principal and the vice-principal were waiting in the foyer for ITN's arrival. They were proud that the college's attitude and facilities had enabled Alexander to achieve. The filming lasted into the afternoon. Mrs Wade had to conduct a typical lesson for the cameras. Alexander was interviewed at length and filmed as he first illegibly planned and then dictated the beginning of an essay. It was exhausting: I had no idea of the work which goes into making three minutes of television.

The next step was to put the case to the governors and this required careful consideration. I thought an open letter to the headmaster with copies to all of them would be the best approach – that way everything would be out in the open.

We outlined Alexander's background through MENSA, GCSE and 'A' level, and explained how studies for the latter had been carried on in addition to his normal school routine. For his degree, however, we asked for the school's cooperation in granting him reduction in his timetable to enable him to remain in the company of his contemporaries during his studies. We stressed our flexibility and desire to take his teachers' advice on which subjects he should pursue. We said that that we would welcome the opportunity of speaking to the governors in person when they came to consider the request, so that we could clarify any queries that might arise.

With Winchester out of the running, and the response from Alexander's school far from certain, it seemed that the only responsible thing to do would be to research as many alternatives for entry at 13+ as possible. We wrote for prospectuses from independent schools within driving distance. In due course these arrived, with the customary compliments note attached.

One, however, stood out. It was from Mr Robert Hardy, the then headmaster of Milton Abbey School, near Blandford Forum in Dorset. It contained a personal letter saying how much he would like to meet us to discuss the possibility of Alexander coming to the school. Later it transpired that he had seen Andrew and Alexander on television and our name rang a bell. We made an appointment for them to meet him in mid October.

During the wait for the governors' reply, the headmaster gave me a written indication of what their decision was likely to be. He said that as matters of principle had been raised, the governors would have to decide whether granting a 50 per cent reduction in Alexander's timetable to allow him to study for a degree might set a precedent which, in the context of the school, it might not be proper to authorise.

I only hoped that the governors' decision would not correspond with his prediction of their thoughts: unfortunately, this was not the case. As a concession, though, he could stop attending English lessons from half term.

The letter announcing this arrived the day before the trip to Milton Abbey and left our thoughts in complete turmoil. With a virtually full timetable and the consequent home work, it would be impossible for Alexander to do his degree. We talked into the early hours and concluded that the only chance would be to put a truly unconventional proposal to Mr Robert Hardy. Our request would be to adapt Alexander's timetable to allow him to do his degree, and to take him at the age of twelve instead of thirteen.

Alexander fell in love with the school, which is set in rolling Dorset landscape. It has a fourteenth century abbey with a great and glorious Pugin stained glass window. The dining room has a superb carved ceiling, and elegant wooden chairs donated by former pupils. Mr Hardy did not bat an eyelid at our proposals, but made careful notes throughout the interview – he was making a real effort to understand Alexander's needs and communicated to us a positive interest in accommodating him. Issues, such as the virtual inevitability of someone as different as Alexander being a target for victimisation and how that should be handled – were tackled head on at his instigation.

It was difficult to know on their return which one of them was the more excited. Andrew was impressed with the open nature of Mr Hardy's response; the general ambience of the school with its small classes of about eight boys, in which each had the opportunity to flourish as an individual; and its highly sympathetic attitude towards dyslexia. As well being impressed by these things, they came back with tales of the window in the abbey, having recently seen the Pugin exhibition at the Victoria and Albert Museum. Alexander greatly appreciated Mr Hardy's efforts to get to know his prospective pupils. He also took great glee in the novelty of the tuck shop where delights as diverse as books, chocolate and tea and toast could be purchased.

Two days later we received a letter formalising the discussions which had been held, indicating the school's serious consideration of Alexander, asking for reports and any other information that might be of use that could further clarify the position, and confirmation of his request for a second interview early in December, this time with me present as well. We dispatched everything we had at hand, including a copy of the essay on William Jay Smith's poem in order to illustrate not just his difficulties, but what he could actually achieve.

I believed at this point that the explanation that I had given to Alexander's headmaster about my comments to the press had put the matter to rest. I was therefore somewhat alarmed to receive another letter on this subject, this time saying that I had caused offence to the staff and asking now their annoyance could be dispelled. In reply I made it clear that I would welcome the opportunity of addressing the governors, both to dispel any misleading impressions caused by certain teachers' interpretation of my remarks, and to support the comments I actually had made, provided that I could be given specific details of any accusations, but to these suggestions I received no response.

On December 3rd we visited Milton Abbey. It was confirmed that the school would welcome him as a pupil in September 1995 to study for his degree and follow a modified curriculum. He would live with the other third formers, but for his Open University studies would be provided with his own room, for which we would supply the necessary tape and video recorders, radio and television. After all we had been through, I found it hard to accustom myself to such an accommodating attitude. It was as if we had abruptly landed in a remote paradise where the natives were extremely friendly.

The next educational stage was already in progress. Alexander had met his Open University tutor, Michael Hughes, and during his English lessons went to the school library to make a start on the preparatory reading. In many respects he seemed to enjoy this term, for he was with his friend again, and the lessons were more varied in nature.

The bullying, unfortunately, had resumed a couple of weeks into September, mostly taking place around his locker with boys breaking into it; hiding his books; obstructing him when he tried to reach it; and hitting him when he tried to sort out what he needed to take home at the end of the day. As Andrew waited for him in the car he used to fume with frustration as Alexander emerged, later and later each day. He knew that while he was sitting there, our son was being beaten up. He felt that it was imperative not to breach the divide between the roles of parent and teacher, march in, and rescue the victim. It would only give the bullies another excuse to torment Alexander. I approached his tutor, twice in writing, and as a consequence, the bullying abated somewhat.

The problem nevertheless remained of how Alexander could possibly cope with his degree on top of all the school work during the two terms before he started at Milton Abbey. I had written again to the governors asking them to reconsider their decision, but to no avail. The only solution that we kept coming back to was to remove him from school for that period. The degree would be his real education.

The stress involved in making this decision was enormous. We were particularly concerned about the legality of the situation, but Andrew consulted the Education Act. It states quite clearly that all children over five must receive education appropriate to their age, ability and any special needs: interestingly, the word 'school' is not mentioned in this context. As teachers we had naturally hoped that schooling and education could be allowed to take place in the same building. Indeed, that had been one reason to turn to the Open – rather than a conventional – University. It was ironic that we were going to have to contemplate removing him, if only temporarily, from school altogether. We procrastinated to the last moment, and then, at the end of term, wrote to the headmaster informing him that Alexander would not be returning in January. It was done. We felt much better, especially when we received his end of term report. In the activities section, beneath a heavy layer of correction fluid, was writing which, when held up to the light, read: 'Open University Studies in English'. Clearly, such an acknowledgement had been the subject of official disapproval. The concluding comment, ignoring the degree level work that

Alexander was pursuing instead of his English lessons, suggested that the time could be used improving the skills required to combat his considerable technical difficulties. Charitably interpreted, this represented a complete lack of understanding, but I saw in the light of the non-person treatment his grandfather had received during his years of exile, when his books had been burned by the Nazis and pulped by the Communists.

Thought had to be given to the structure of Alexander's week. After all, he couldn't just sit at home every day, so a pattern developed which, with variations, went like this:

Monday. He worked at home.

Tuesday. He worked at home in the morning, then walked (45 minutes) to my parents' house where he would spend the night, being collected for an hour's tutorial on a Victorian theme in the evening by Dr Paul Dean.

Wednesday. Alexander would spend the morning with my parents before walking home after lunch and working in the afternoon.

Thursday. He worked at home.

Friday. He came to college with me and read in the library for the morning. In the afternoon I took him swimming. To my amazement he has turned from a non swimmer to having the confidence to manage a length of the pool.

Saturday. Work at home.

Sunday. Trip to London.

My parents made a great fuss of Alexander during his weekly visits. My father, whose intelligence and dry wit he really enjoys, would record old black and white films during the week that they would watch together late on Tuesday evenings. My mother would make him all his favourite meals, indulging him with delicacies that he would not be allowed on a daily basis at home. They shared our concerns about his removal from school, but once it was accomplished made every effort to support his physical and emotional well-being, not to mention funding his course and buying his books.

Until the degree started in February I felt I had to account for exactly what he did each day, so Emily donated a jungle book notepad and I kept a record – here as an example is the first week's entry:

January 1995: Week 1

Monday 2nd: Tate Gallery – Whistler Exhibition.

Tuesday 3rd: Best pp. 19–40 + Victorian discussion with Dr Dean.

Wednesday 4th: Best pp. 40–53 + Gombrich pp. 3–24.

Thursday 5th: Best pp. 53–69.

Friday 6th: Briggs pp. 11–20 + swimming.

Saturday 7th: Best pp. 69–73 + V & A museum including Morris room + during the course of the week the whole of Evelyn Waugh's *Brideshead Revisited* on tape.

The books referred to are Geoffrey Best's *Mid-Victorian Britain*, Asa Briggs' *Victorian Cities* and Sir Ernst Gombrich's *The Story of Art*.

Alexander's experience of the Open University has been like a dream come true. Proper allowance has been made for his disabilities, and all the material has been provided on tape for the course units themselves and, from the Royal National Institute for the Blind, the books which constitute the essential reading. We didn't know about the latter provision, which is why, in the typical week shown above, he was only reading a few sides each day. Now, with everything on tape, he can 'read' at an acceptable pace, and without undue stress.

As with my offer to meet the governors to discuss Alexander's curriculum, there had been no response to my suggestion to do the same over the matter of the publicity, nor was I given details of the various interpretations placed on my comments. As several months had gone by, I assumed the details were not going to be forthcoming and the whole matter was to be allowed to die a dignified death – not so! It was held back until I was in a vulnerable position – regarding Emily – at the time when decisions were made over which children to allow to progress from the pre-prep to the lower school. In practice parents are not involved in this process as the heads of the two schools discuss each pupil and virtually all are offered places. We had no worries about Emily. She was a model pupil: all her reports had been excellent; she was in the top maths set, was an avid and accurate reader, and was praised for her vocabulary, control over punctuation and beautiful presentation.

It therefore seemed like the beginning of a hideous and unjust nightmare when I received a letter from her prospective headmaster inquiring if we would be kind enough to share with him our plans for the next stage of Emily's education. He remarked that it occurred to him that certain misgivings we had voiced from time to time during Alexander's period in the school might have prompted us to consider an alternative for Emily's future, and that if that was the case, the school would respect our decision, knowing it to have been reached after very careful consideration. If however, we did want Emily to attend the lower school, there were a number of issues which would have to be addressed. I was upset that Alexander's difficulties and sufferings were going to be used against his sister, who had never given any one cause for concern. I replied asking for her to be considered in the normal manner, in her own right, there being no parallels between Alexander and Emily's educational expectations. I said that if he specifically wanted to discuss Emily, then we would be more than willing to see him, but stressed that as Alexander was not even a pupil at the school, we were not prepared to link the two in discussion.

This produced a response which revealed the previously hidden agenda in its full colours – it was not Emily's future, but my media utterances (which he described as regrettable and unrepresentative) that had yet to be resolved. The two were to be linked and written assurances sought from me.

I cried when I read this missive, for how could I betray my son's sufferings by denying the reasons I had helped him to find the path to success, in a trade-off for an offer of a place for Emily, who, considered on her own merits, would have no need for what I considered to be such underhand dealings? Can one child's future be compromised at the expense of another's? Despair and frustration turned to anger at what I saw as the injustice of the situation, an anger which perhaps only a mother can feel when she sees one of her children threatened. This was the mood in which I approached the interview with the headmaster: Emily was offered a place.

The Open University accepted his working method of tape and transcript. Special arrangements have been made for him to have regular individual meetings with his tutor, Mr Hughes, once a month. It was not considered advisable for him to attend the seminars and summer school as it was thought that the presence of a precocious twelve-year-old might be off-putting to those who had perhaps just returned to education after a long gap.

Mr Hughes was an ideal choice as tutor for Alexander. He took great pains to understand the nature of his dyslexic difficulties and, with these effectively understood and placed to one side, as it were, the two struck up an excellent, amicable but suitably formal relationship, which is in my view exactly what is needed. Always helpful and attentive to the necessary detail, Mr Hughes has made the first year of study on the Arts Foundation Course a treat for us all. Alexander's inability to write has never been an issue and Mr Hughes was able to see instantly beyond this problem, directly into the true quality of his mind.

In his early essays, Alexander's mark rose from 80 per cent to begin with on History, to 88 per cent on English Literature, and a staggering 100 per cent on Art History. We couldn't believe our eyes when this last essay was returned – well, it justified all those trips to London, and also gave us an even clearer indication of where Alexander's true interests and talents lay.

I am genuinely pleased that this ability is not in a subject in which I can claim any expertise. I suppose that my gift to Alexander was teaching him how to think. I am no longer his teacher officially or unofficially – the learning is now entirely his responsibility, although we do spend time helping him organise himself.

The Open University represents for Alexander a level playing field where he can study on equal terms with other students. As a rule, life is not usually so straightforward for dyslexics: it is an uphill marathon where all the odds are stacked against them without any consideration as to whether this might be fair, sensible, or even of any productive use. We were amazed when Alexander achieved full marks in the History of Art essay, but we should not have been surprised. After all, it merely represented what he was capable of when all the obstacles in the great sack race of life, in which he had previously competed – quite literally – with a handicap, were suddenly removed. That is what the Open University is, I believe, for thousands of other students: it is an institution designed not to perpetuate inequalities. In its policy statement, the Open University alludes specifically to race, gender, sexual orientation, age, occupation, marital status, sensory or physical disability, religious or other beliefs as factors that will *not* stand in the way of students, and that is exactly, in our experience, how things really are.

Alexander is now a true companion. Intellectually he is not a child, and with patience he will explain philosophical concepts or matters arising from world history or politics which are outside my scope. We no longer have disagreements over censorship. He has his own television which, like the master system, he saved up for, and is his own self-regulating body, holding strong views on sexual exploitation and gratuitous violence. His stomach is, however, stronger than mine, and he is the one who tells me when I can come out from behind the cushion once a particularly blood-spurting incident in *Bramwell* is over! I will miss him terribly when he goes to Milton Abbey this autumn, but I recognise that as well as his intellectual development, he needs the social integration provided by a caring school environment.

The best man at our wedding, Dr Paul Katona, gave us the following advice in his address at the reception: 'Be unconventional – but first learn the conventions. Then you can break them.' I had no idea at the time how apposite his statement would become.

Alexander's Account:

At the end of my last year in the lower school I went to see Mr Taylor, the head of English at Winchester College. The atmosphere was very friendly and, as the interview progressed, he seemed to become more and more convinced that I was suitable for the College. At the end of the meeting I thought it was not a case of if I could come, but how I could be accommodated. He said that he would speak to the headmaster on our behalf, and as I left the house and crossed the street, my father cried out: 'Yes! You've charmed him!' I felt as I had done on the day I had had the GCSE results, that is, triumphant *in excelsis*.

The day after the end of term, I set off on holiday to Budapest with my father. It was the first time I had gone anywhere abroad without my mother. Although this absence was to be a short one, I felt it to be symbolic of a new phase in my life, a phase of greater independence. I was both excited and sad at the prospect, for I would be on my own. Most of my knowledge had come from her and emotional development through that knowledge. Up until then my mother had been a sort of buffer for me – something soft to land on, and break the fall when I felt depressed from what was happening at school. She was to me a source of stability and certainty, but now she has encouraged me to develop a character which isn't reliant on her for intellectual stimulus. My OU studies are bringing out my personality and developing it, so that I have a thirst for knowledge which I can't satisfy immediately by asking her. Now I have to find out for myself.

While I was in Budapest, I not only developed my interest in art further by speaking to my grandfather, and discussing illustrations and reproductions of paintings, by Hieronymous Bosch in particular, but I also became interested in architecture. This was encouraged by my frequent trips to museums, and also by looking at the medieval castle at Visegrád and the summer palace nearby. I began to feel almost like a native, and by the time I left, I felt a true Hungarian as a result of living in the cosmopolitan, continental environment of my grandfather's apartment overlooking the Danube. Here I not only asked him about history, but found a unique field to explore, that of philosophy, which, I discovered, was not a mere question of analysing ideology, but of formulating ideas and justifying them, without resorting to base material proof. By this I mean an intellectual verity is achieved which is metaphysical – using the mind instead of the physical world to prove a theory.

In the airplane when I was flying alone back to England, I was interested to discover that I had been placed next to an American dyslexia specialist. From my conversation with her I was able to understand the reasons behind conventional treatments for dyslexia and see how inappropriate they would have been if applied to me. Thinking about this made me realise how lucky I was that my parents had chosen to concentrate on my own specialities.

A few weeks after my return, I discovered that I would not be able to go to Winchester College. This upset me greatly, as emotionally, while in the exciting atmosphere of Budapest, I had finally been able to renounce my role of outcast as defined by my school environment.

The rest of that summer was not all doom and gloom: for August was the month in which I passed my 'A' level in English Literature. On the day, I went to Fareham College and was interviewed by two local television stations. After the long session with photographers, representing most of the major daily papers, we returned home to discover, looking at the local newspaper, that I was front page news with a picture that had been taken on the previous day. I was shown balancing precariously on a pile of books, holding a copy of *Our Mutual Friend* in one hand and raising the other in a clenched fist representative of victory. I remember the incident very clearly, since the shot took well over an hour, while the photographer had placed me in many bizarre poses, in one of which I was made to balance, yogi style, on volumes of the *Encyclopaedia Britannica*, a tape in my mouth, a book in one hand, and a tape recorder in the other. After resting in the garden for a few hours, I went off to an interview on Meridian, and that night we drank most of the rest of the Spanish Cava and generally enjoyed ourselves.

This was not the end of the celebrations. My parents organised a party. I felt in a way that my surroundings didn't exist, as if I was floating on a cloud, not just representative of my high elation, but of the intellectual enjoyment the 'A' level had given me. Everyone who was able to come, as my father remarked in his speech, had made some contribution to the success that we were celebrating. The people who were there ranged from my understanding lower school music teacher to my father's oldest friend, and my sister's youngest. My bubble did not burst for a long time afterwards. For several days I received cards from many people including my Art teacher in the lower school (who had always encouraged me, in spite of my lack of ability in her subject) and friends of my parents and grandparents.

With the new term came the familiar story. As after my GCSE, I was bubbling inside with the expectation that the school would acknowledge my achievement, and I would somehow belong. At the beginning of term assembly, I thought the head might mention it, but when I realised, as other people's successes were listed, that mine wasn't going to be, I was overcome with a sadness which made me think that the school regarded me as unimportant – that I was just a scab which should be flicked off at the earliest opportunity.

For the first two weeks, boys wanted to know and be associated with me, shake my hand and be amongst the first to offer congratulations. But then, things got back to normal, or rather to the traditional routine, except slightly varied this time, for here was a new environment which gave occasion to different methods of bullying and harassment, as well as the usual opportunities offered by sport. In this part of the school we had lockers: mine was regularly broken into and my books taken, along with my laboratory coat and various other articles. Sometimes things were hidden for a couple of days, and then their mysterious return would make me look foolish. After school, I would be attacked in the vicinity of the lockers.

When my mother complained to my tutor I was summoned in front of her with the bullies. They thronged together, concocting the usual potion of lies: it hadn't been them, or I had been over reacting, and I couldn't take a joke. I felt that the blame rubbed off on me, and I was told by my tutor not to be over sensitive. She told us that we must all live in the community together. Even though she didn't expect us to be bosom buddies, she wanted us all to get on with each other. My tormentors, though, did seem to have been scared by the experience and the thought of being summoned again, but the bullying was never stamped out completely, and I was still taunted about deficiencies in my physical ability.

During the autumn term, my parents applied for my timetable to be reduced by 50 per cent, but the request was turned down, although I was allowed to be excused English lessons on the grounds that I had already passed 'A' level in the subject. We sent off to various independent schools for brochures, and received their prospectuses, most importantly one from Milton Abbey in Dorset with a personal note from the headmaster inviting us there.

I fell in love with the school as we drove down a winding lane which gave me a panorama of the countryside and the glorious russet and brown leaves on the trees that banked the roadside. I instantly felt at home from the moment that I got out of the car: here I felt that I slotted into an empty place, not just in my feelings, but practically as well.

The school has accepted me, not for what they want me to be, but for what I am. They are willing to allow me to be an individual. They have understood that my needs are different from those of my age group, yet have arranged an integration which accommodates me. When I saw this approach, I felt incredibly surprised, not knowing that such liberal-mindedness could exist within the system of education in this country. But that was not the only important thing that stood out: for the first time in many years, I felt accepted as part of a community.

Because of my own school's refusal to grant me the timetable concession, and with my course starting in February, my parents withdrew me at the end of the autumn term. On the last day, I went to find my friend before school began. Because there were so many other people about, I was only able to whisper to him that I was leaving. However, on the way to the cathedral service, I managed to give him the details. We were both upset as we would no longer be able to see each other every day. Perhaps the clearest moment I remember was gazing up at the arch over the main gate, which we were driving through and thinking that this was the end of my time there. My feelings were mixed at this point: there was relief that my future was taking a new direction and regret at what I saw as the school's rejection of what I was. On joining the school, I had hoped to be a model pupil – to form part of it, belong, and be just as essential as the others. But progressively I had felt that the school did not want me – not its individual members, but its character and ethos, which seemed to be that all pupils should conform in excellence *within* its framework, and not one external to it, unless the school could comprehend and accept its terms: this was what my achievements were not and I was not – a part of my life was over.

I felt a little empty in a way, since there was now a gap. I didn't quite realise then how completely it would be filled by my Open University degree.

While writing this book, I am in a period between schools. I have spent my time studying, and my life has become an interesting and constantly evolving routine. I enjoy my degree, and though the work at times is very challenging, the OU has encouraged my mind to explore connections and to make use of everything I learn, not just of tiny and regularly examined fragments of redundant information. It has freed me from such restraints, allowing me to branch out and encompass multiple areas of knowledge. This approach has enabled me to explore Victorian society as a whole – the Crimean War, the Reform Acts and the Industrial Revolution are not just topics in their own right, but contribute to the enormous social change of the time. Now, when I look at a picture I don't see it as a mere matter of conventional symbolism independent of its own time. Instead I look for the influences of contemporary society laid deep into the structure of the painting – for example, in William Holman Hunt's *A Converted British Family Sheltering a Priest from the Persecution of the Druids*, I didn't see an example of high church iconography or a mere 'adven-

ture' story. I perceived it as the expression of a wide range
of contemporary issues such as the re-establishment of the
Catholic church in England and the growing non-conform-
ist movements, who were constantly in fear of being wiped
out by the larger groups. I was also able to make use of things
that I have learned in the past for the 'A' level such as figural
significance in relation to things such as the bullrushes in
the corner, symbolic of the story of Moses being hidden
from his oppressors, just as God is sheltering this family. I
am happy because I am no longer restricted and my whole
mind is brought into play.

Once a month I have a tutorial with Mr Hughes – I find
this contact re-assuring, for as I don't attend the same
sessions as the other students, it lets me know that I am on
course with my studies. When I first met Mr Hughes, I was
a bit nervous, in case he was like my school teachers who
picked up on my spellings, but he turned out to be very open
minded, wanting to know about my methods rather than
telling me how things were conventionally done. This was
not as a mere formality of approach, but a genuine interest
to see how my mind worked. In the tutorials he has shown
me angles of approach without telling me what to think. His
kindness and confidence in me as a student have reinforced
my ability for independent thought.

I don't spend all my time at home. I walk down to my
grandparents once a week, and back again after staying the
night. I will treasure the time I have been able to spend with
them this year – it is an experience of pure relaxation and
happiness. Granny used to be a City Councillor, and we
devote hours to discussing all the local political issues over
late night snacks in the kitchen. I love her favourite stories
of war time adventures as a VAD in Africa – they give me a
deeper insight into her personality. With Grandad I discuss

classic black and white films, trading favourite catch phrases or incidents. He saves gems that will be of particular interest to me from the newspapers and we talk about the unusual and amusing items from the week's news. I look on their house as a second home. I have my own bedroom – which used to be my mother's when she was a girl. They have decorated it for me with cuttings from when I joined MENSA onwards. On Tuesdays I also spend an hour with Dr Paul Dean. I have known him for half my life. When I was six, I liked his immediately apparent sense of humour and wonderful way of dealing with children. His comical phrases were amusing to me on one level, and intellectually interesting in another. I could see there was complex thought behind the humour. I didn't always understand it but I knew it was there and would be something I could share more fully as I grew older. Now it is the wide range and interdisciplinary scope of his mind that inspires me. He is able to provide a complete overview of a topic: for example, he introduced me to the connections between the Lady of Shalott and various pre-Raphaelite paintings which in their turn are both part of and expressions of the cultural make-up of the Victorian society that we have been studying. He awakens in me a great curiosity, and when I leave his house I feel excited and filled with the desire to find out more.

At the weekends we visit art galleries and museums in London, my favourite being the National Gallery, where my father and I have systematically gone through every room, and we have only to finish the basements. My field is no longer exclusively literature, but is turning more and more to Art History, my essay on which earned me 100 per cent from my Open University tutor. The Open University has filled the gap which existed in me for so many years, and now I have a focus to my life, or if you like, a framework, on which I can build.

This chapter may have seemed like a conclusion in itself, bringing events up to the present moment, but I would like to sum up how things have changed completely for me. Walking down to my grandparents' house a few weeks ago in the mild warmth of early summer, I suddenly experienced a great rush of energy, not physical or mental, but perhaps a mixture of the two: I felt free in a way I hadn't before: free of the ropes which tie intellectual thought down in a dyslexic – the concentration on letter formation, writing and spelling. It's my mind which can work, rather than my hands which can't. I use my mouth and not my pen. I am happier now than I have ever been before in my twelve years of existence.

CHAPTER SEVEN

A Little Edge of Darkness

Alexander's story is far from over, but this is a good point to break the narrative and reflect on what has been achieved, as well as what lies ahead.

When he was very small, his Hungarian grandfather predicted that he would be capable of remarkable conversation when he actually learned to speak. However, only a few people outside our family circle have had the requisite qualities to understand our son fully. They include: Mrs Elisabeth Wade, whose dedicated professionalism over a sustained period has assisted Alexander's development; Mr Michael Hughes, his Open University tutor, whose sensitive handling of everything has made the first year of study a pleasure, not only for Alexander, but for us as well; Mr Robin Freeland, the educational psychologist, whose initial diagnosis contained the vital observation that he would become frustrated if it were not possible for him to achieve his potential; Dr Paul Dean, who recognised the nature and scope of that potential and has advised, admired, supported, and more recently, tutored him; and Mr Robert Hardy, headmaster of Milton Abbey, who had the flexibility to admit him to a school where he could be with his contemporaries and continue his degree course.

Perhaps our lives might have been more convenient if we had given in to conventional expectations of how Alexander should progress. We could have spent years working on his handwriting and spelling. We could have expended all his energy in attempting to unpick the Gordian knot, when in fact it was so much better to cut it instead. Because *dyslexia cannot be 'cured'*, in the end we never 'solved' his problems. We circumvented them instead, so that eventually it became accepted that his primary input was through his ears, and his output was, via his mouth, on to tape.

But it was hard, especially when we were told, often rather condescendingly, by people in influential positions, what was right for our son. It was difficult to contradict, and to insist that we instinctively knew best, especially in a period in history in which there was considerable pressure to conform – eccentricity and stepping out of line were simply not tolerated. However, we determined to be unconventional. No other way open to us could possibly have succeeded.

In a nutshell, the path we chose made it possible to liberate Alexander from the prison of his dyslexia. Nobody – let alone a dyslexic – had ever passed English 'A' level at the age of eleven. Just because something has not been done before does not mean that it cannot be done in the future. As George Bernard Shaw said, 'Some men see things as they are, and say "why?"; I dream of things that never were, and say, "why not?"'

The result is that Alexander can look forward to the future with confidence. Instead of wasting all his time and energy in a pointless struggle with spelling in which the odds are stacked against him, he can complete his degree course in wonderful surroundings. With luck, by then, the voice sensitive word processor will be commercially available. This will enable him to function independently of us. It will also make life easier for thousands of other people with problems similar to his.

If this book has any 'message' at all, it is to dyslexics and others with disabilities. They know from experience that the world is not an accommodating place, and that to get anywhere they have to work harder than the rest.

Well, 'tis morning. Alexander will soon be off to Dorset to embark on a new and exciting stage of his life. And I, too, think I can see a little edge of darkness just beginning to steal away from the window pane.

The Slumbers
of the Sleeping Stars

The following selection of Alexander's poetry was written largely just before his eighth birthday, although *Poetry Itself, The End of All Ends, Opposition Strategy* and *The Imprisonment of Persephone* were all written between March and June of 1991 when he was eight years old.

The Slumbers of the Sleeping Stars

As I lie in my bed
I listen to the stars singing
I think of novels and things I've heard
As the music of the stars
> Drifts
> Down
> Upon
> Me.

The sun-shining stars sing and dance
In my mind and in the sky
And then I fall asleep
With the knowledge of the stars
And their joy
> Sweeping
> Down
> Upon
> Me.

The Birds

Birds fly in the high sky
Where there is nothing but emptiness and clouds
Gracefully they soar through the air
Twisting turning looping the loop.

Feathers pricked flapping faster they flee
For danger approaches: the hunters are on the prowl
Bullets fly: Birds flutter and fall
The survivors flee from the firing.

The Sky's Beauty

The Evening's glory gives us
No need for fear
The stars pattern the sky
And the sweet sound of night-time dawns
No light can spoil this delicate beauty
As Flowers blossom the sky does with stars
And the moon casts its light upon this wonder
When the Morning ascends this glory retreats
And the Sun casts its light upon the shadowed day.

The Barriers of Night and Day

Sunlight is spreading over the world
The day is rough and hot
As trees spread their leaves in the hot sun
They show that some of their great glory has faded.

When the darkness comes, cool and satisfactory
Tones sing in the air.
The tranquillity of this peaceful hour
Rains/Reigns over the world.

The Shark's Trap

A shark's wondrous teeth search the Ocean
Fish swim into this trap
They have no defence but their simple selves
But then the shark finds himself in a trap
As fishermen cast their nets
And as he had no rescue he is left to die
His skin will be thrown away
And his flesh will be devoured upon this
                                    FATAL DAY

Sleep

Sleep is the bus stop to unconsciousness
And into this great abyss they fall
Treading on paths untrodden before,
Losing their way, at each corner
        They plunge
        Deeper and further
        Into their minds.

Poetry Itself

Poetry is a form of compassion
Which: describes, amuses, pleases
And sets examples to the world.
These ambitions are mixed
        To make a form
Whose images are so divine
        That all populations
                celebrate
                this
        Glorious pattern
                of
        feelings.

The Life of the Flowers

Roses flower in Spring and Summer
Dew drops fall
Blue bells ring
Alas it is Autumn: flowers wither
The sting
Of Winter
Kills.

Opposition Strategy

'ORDER,' the Speaker shouts
As politicians raise their voices
In protest against the Government's decision.

Waving their order papers they yell
'The Government is off its head:
It will never win another election.'

The main opposition leader speaks out in
Condemnation: 'How much is this proposal
Going to cost our country?'

A back bench MP screams across the chamber –
'Has the Right Honourable gentleman
Considered the effects of this proposal?'

And so the rabble between the two sides
Of the House continues forever in political
Triumph and loss in past present and future.

The End of all Ends

Fumes are in the air
As electricity plants work their horrid engines.
Buses along the road make the air smell foul
And people drink polluted water and
Die for acid rain fills the air
And sewage makes the beaches unsafe
And tourists flee from them.

And on the pleasant beaches of
Asia birds suffer and die from oil spills –
More and more are slain each day
Until their species disevolves.
A Fateful day will come when ALL THINGS WILL
                                            FADE
And Man, the most developed of all species, will
                                          confess
That his kind has killed the world.

The Imprisonment of Persephone

In the underworld stirs a mist
As Hades, dark king of this inhospitable abode,
Plans the capture of Persephone.

He sweeps her down as a wind plucking grass.
In discontentment she lives in darkness cruel
Tortured with hunger and withered in soul.

On the great mount of Olympus stands Zeus.
The king of the Gods admires his great empire –
Angered, he orders Persephone's release.

On the wings of Hermes she rejoices her freedom
Ascending from Tartarean heat and Elysian beauty
She is embraced in the arms of Demeter.